Write It Right

The Ground Rules® for Self-Editing Like the Pros

Dawn Josephson
&
Lauren Hidden

Published by
Ground Rules Press
A subsidiary of
Cameo Publications, LLC
©2005

03 04 05 06 HH 10 9 8 7 6 5 4 3 2 1
Printed in the United States of America
ISBN: 0-97449662-6
BISAC: REF026000
REFERENCE / Writing Skills
$17.95 US Funds
Library of Congress: 2005925809
Published by Ground Rules Press a subsidary
of Cameo Publications, LLC

Cover and interior design by David Josephson, Copyright © 2005
of Cameo Publications

Author photos by Bill Littell, IWL Photography,
Hilton Head Island, SC

Requests for permission to make copies of any part of this work can be made to:

Ground Rules Press
PO Box 8006
Hilton Head Island, SC 29938
1-866-372-2636
info@masterwritingcoach.com
www.masterwritingcoach.com

Look What the Pros are Saying About
Write It Right...

"It's finally here – a book on editing your writing that relies on real-world examples and usage. Simple, easy, powerful. Read it and you'll write better forever."

— Pam Lontos, President
PR/PR Public Relations

"*Write It Right* takes the mystery out of the self-editing process. A well-organized and valuable tool for every author."

— Kathryn R. Wall, author
The Bay Tanner mysteries

"This is a 'must have' book for anyone who wants to improve their writing. Its appendix alone, with its quick grammar and usage tips, make *Write It Right* well worth the price."

— Dick Bruso, branding expert and
Founder of Heard Above the Noise

"Once I picked up this book and started to read, I was hooked! Dawn Josephson and Lauren Hidden have written a book that outlines the essential steps for successfully self-editing any written work. I highly recommend it."

— Simon Warwick-Smith, President
Warwick Associates, Publishing Consultants

"I see so much bad writing, and it can ruin my impression of the author. Get help if you're not sure. Read this book for starters!"

— David DeKok, author
Unseen Danger: A Tragedy of People, Government,
and the Centralia Mine Fire

"As a teacher of writing, I can't wait to give my kids some of these ideas so they can be years ahead in their studies!"

— Susan E. Cambron
Language Arts Teacher

Dedication

~~To all those writers who have anguished over fine tuning and editing their own writing.~~

~~To all those who have rewritten their own work in an attempt to write well.~~

~~To everyone who has struggled with self-editing.~~

~~To anyone who has struggled to write and edit better.~~

To anyone who has ever struggled to *write it right*.

Contents

Acknowledgments
- ☑ From Lauren Hidden.................................... xiii
- ☑ From Dawn Josephson xv

Introduction **15**
- ☑ The Writing Two-Step 16
- ☑ The Case for Self-Editing 16
- ☑ Editing 101 17
- ☑ Why We Wrote This Book.......................17
- ☑ How This Book is Organized 18
- ☑ The Race to the Finish Line......................18

Step One: The Warm Up Search for the Occurrence of Similar Writing Challenges
Knowing Your Problems is Half the Battle........21
- ☑ Past, Present, and Future 22
- ☑ The Ground Rules...................................23
- ☑ Some Real-Life Samples..........................25
- ☑ Test Yourself...33
- ☑ How Did You Do?..................................37
- ☑ Scoring...44
- ☑ Frequently Asked Questions....................45
- ☑ Key Points 46
- ☑ Turning Points –
  Questions for Self-Reflection 47

Step Two: Approach the Starting Line Prepare to Edit
Preparation Makes Perfect.............................51
- ☑ Think Like an Editor, not a Writer...............51
- ☑ The Ground Rules...................................53
- ☑ Some Real-Life Samples...........................55

☑ Frequently Asked Questions 60
☑ Key Points 61
☑ Turning Points –
    Questions for Self-Reflection 62

Step Three: Run the Race
The Editing Process Begins
Going for the Long Haul **67**

☑ Set the Course for Success 68
☑ The Ground Rules 69
☑ The Hand Off 71
☑ Frequently Asked Questions 71
☑ Key Points 72
☑ Turning Points –
    Questions for Self-Reflection 73

Step Four: Hand Off the Baton
Let the Relay Begin
Use Your Team to Get Ahead **77**

☑ You Can Get By with a Little Help
    from Your Friends 77
☑ The Ground Rules 78
☑ Some Real-Life Samples 80
☑ Frequently Asked Questions 83
☑ Key Points 84
☑ Turning Points –
    Questions for Self-Reflection 85

Step Five: A Picture Perfect Finish
The Final Stretch

Closing Thoughts 91
☑ The Ground Rule for the
    Last Leg of the Race 91

☑ Consider Your Accomplishments 92
☑ Cross the Finish Line 93
☑ Frequently Asked Questions 93
☑ Key Points 94
☑ Turning Points – ....
   Questions for Self-Reflection 95

Appendices **99**

Appendix A:
What To Do When You're Pressed for Time ..101
☑ The Ground Rules 101

Appendix B:
How To Sabotage Your Self-Editing Efforts... 103
☑ The Ground Rules 103
☑ What is Grammar? 105

Appendix C:
The Ground Rules of Grammer and Usage ... 105

Appendix D: Forms and Checklists **121**
☑ Example Self-Editing Checklist 121

Epilogue **127**

Index **129**

About Dawn Josephson **133**

About Lauren Hidden **135**

Write It Right

Right

The Ground Rules® for Self-Editing Like the Pros

Acknowledgments

From Lauren Hidden:

I've always wanted to write a book. What I never realized is how many people are required to produce one. From conception to the final product, many talented people have lent their time and expertise. With this in mind, I would like to thank the following people for helping me achieve my dream:

To my parents, Frank and Barbara Davis, thank you for everything; from the happy and stable home you provided, to Dad constantly correcting my grammar and Mom asking, "What, are you writing a book or something?" when I'd get too nosey. You must have seen this book coming! Thanks for your love and encouragement.

My husband, Ed Hidden. Thank you for supporting all my careers: from a social worker to a stay-at-home-mom to an entrepreneur and an author. Thank you for encouraging me to pursue my dreams. I love you.

My sons, Kyle and Andrew Hidden. You are two of the best little boys in the world. Thank you for coming into my life and giving me a new definition of success. I love you "to the moon and back."

My big brothers, Brad Davis and Rob Davis. Thanks for always being there to love and support me. My life would not be the same without you guys.

My best friend, Lisa Heyman, Thank you for encouraging me as a woman, a parent and an entrepreneur. You've shown me extraordinary kindness and love. Friends like you are hard to find.

My co-author, Dawn Josephson. Thank you for being a constant friend, cheerleader and mentor. I can never thank you enough for all you've done for me. From asking me to transcribe a tape many years ago to asking me to co-author a book with you, you have been a continual source of encouragement and inspiration. I've seen your business grow from its humble beginnings to the success it is today. I'm very proud of you.

To the staff at Cameo Publications, David Josephson, Amy Rigard, and Melinda Copp. Thank you for all the help you've given us with this book. From editing and proofreading to design, you've all been key players in the process. You are true professionals.

From Dawn Josephson:

When I first created The Ground Rules® book series and wrote the first book in the series, ***Putting It On Paper: The Ground Rules for Creating Promotional Pieces that Sell Books***, I never thought the response would be as remarkable as it has been. The incredible success of The Ground Rules series has brought me thousands of new friends from all over the world. Their kindness and encouraging words inspired me to have a part in another Ground Rules series book.

Taking on this new writing endeavor would not have been possible without the help of many people. To them I wish to say "thank you."

To my family, thank you for seeing me through yet another project.

To my husband, David Josephson, thank you for your willingness to participate in this project and for your unwavering love and support.

To my co-author, Lauren Hidden, thank you for seeing the vision of this project as clearly as I have. Your expertise has been so valuable every step of the way.

To the staff at Cameo Publications, Melinda Copp and Amy Rigard, thank you for your effort and dedication to making this book what it is.

Finally, to all my friends, both old and new, thank you for your support, your kindness, and your unending desire to master The Ground Rules. You are what make the writing process so rewarding.

Introduction

"I believe more in the scissors than I do in the pencil."
–Truman Capote, American novelist, short story writer, and
playwright

Writing well isn't easy. A 2004 survey by the College Board's National Commission on Writing found that one-third of today's workers do not have appropriate writing skills. This means that many brochures are ineffective, reports are unclear, emails are indecipherable, and writing, in general, is way below par.

If you think this statistic doesn't apply to you because you're not a professional writer or your job is not writing intensive, think again. We are all writers to some extent. Whether you're writing a paper for school, a proposal for work, a resume for a prospective employer, or a letter to a client, you need good writing and editing skills to get your point across.

Still, many people do make their full-time living writing. This includes people who write books and articles, as well as those folks who write instruction manuals, ad copy, catalog descriptions, and anything else that's printed for the world to read. But just because these people write for a living does not mean they know how to write it right. In fact, writing well entails so much more than simply putting words on paper. It's about fine-tuning those words, crystallizing thoughts, eliminating "fluff," and honing the message.

No matter what kind of writing you do or what kind of writer you are, this book will help you refine your writing and editing skills and enable you to put your best foot forward.

The Writing Two-Step

Have you ever wondered why some of your colleagues produce exceptional written documents while yours end up riddled with errors? Are they just natural-born writers? Some of them might be, but more likely than not, those successful writers are really successful self-editors.

Regardless of how much writing you do, you likely fall into the same trap as many other struggling writers. After writing the article, book, brochure, letter, paper, etc., many people breathe a sigh of relief and immediately turn the document in or send it off to clients. If this sounds like you, then realize you're making a huge mistake.

Just because you finished writing the piece does not mean you are done. On the contrary, you've really just begun! Successful writers know that writing is actually a two-step process. Step one is writing the piece, and step two is self-editing it.

Self-editing is a crucial step in the writing process—one that many writers miss. But to increase your chances of being published or getting your message across, you need to self-edit every piece you create.

The Case for Self-Editing

"What? Edit my own work? Isn't that what an editor is for?"

Well, yes and no. An editor's job is to polish your work to ensure your message comes across clearly. But an editor needs an "almost finished" product to work with; he or she is not supposed to rewrite your work. Plus, an editor's time is limited. If your editor has to spend a lot of time refocusing your piece, he or she will have less time to perfect your piece, or may just reject it.

Think of it this way: If an editor has a choice of two writers—one who turns in an "almost perfect" piece and another who turns in a very rough first draft—who do you think the editor will call when the next assignment comes up? Or, if you're sending your written materials to clients, which will they pick—the sales pitch that is compelling or the one that is unclear? In either case, the choice is obvious.

Editing 101

Don't you wish you had paid more attention during your grammar and composition classes? Many of us do. But even if you had, would you really remember all those thousands of rules? Let's face it, grammar is hard and it takes a long time to master usage and style.

Fortunately, you don't have to re-take college-level writing and grammar courses or buy a three-inch thick grammar book to improve your self-editing skills. You don't even need to be able to recite the difference between simple past tense and past perfect progressive tense. You simply need to identify your writing challenges (in real world language) and know how to eliminate them in the editing process. That's what this book will show you.

The challenge for many people is that most grammar guides give definitions of every possible part of speech, its rules of use, and sentence examples that regular people would never use in modern writing. This is not to say that grammar guides are useless. They most certainly have their purpose: to look up something you have a question about, not as a tool to help self-edit your writing.

That's why this book is not a style guide; it's not a thesaurus, or a dictionary, or even a grammar book! This is a book you use after you've written your piece. It describes a simple five-step self-editing process that will add sparkle and pizzazz to your writing in no time. The tools in this book will teach you how to focus in on your own specific writing challenges and overcome them in the editing process.

Will it take some work on your part? Of course! Nothing worthwhile is ever easy. But this process will get quicker over time, and your payoff will be enormous.

Why We Wrote This Book

After working with hundreds of people to help them enhance their writing, we found that self-editing intimidates most people. They revealed that flashbacks of college and high school papers riddled with red ink and indecipherable grammar rules filled their mind. These people desperately wanted to improve their writing, but they thought the task of self-editing was insurmountable.

We knew we could improve their work by doing their editing for them, but that didn't solve the long-term problem. It reminded us of the old saying, "Give a man a fish and he eats for a day. Teach a man to fish and he eats for a lifetime." We wanted to do more than simply give people an edited piece of work; we wanted to show them a painless process for self-editing that would enhance their skills for a lifetime and make them more marketable in today's fiercely competitive business environment.

Knowing that most people don't understand grammar guides, nor do they even want to understand them, we developed this simple five-step process that focuses on the individual's unique challenges rather than rule memorization. We found that by making the editing process personalized for people, they actually "got it" and followed it to the letter (no pun intended). The more they practiced the process, the quicker self-editing became, and the stronger their writing was from word one. It's this process that has worked for hundreds of people that we're sharing with you now.

The word "process" is important. As you go through the steps in this book, you will be able to create your own, individualized process for self-editing. Then, as you improve your self-editing skills, you will no longer have to actually "do" the process any longer. The steps will become a subconscious part of your writing routine. They'll be as natural to you as breathing, and you'll soon wonder what all the fuss was about self-editing in the first place.

How This Book is Organized

As you read the following pages, you'll notice some distinctive sections along the way. Each is there to guide you and help you create your own self-editing process. In each chapter you'll see Ground Rules for the specific step; Real-Life Samples (when appropriate) that will illustrate the Ground Rules in Action; Turning Points, which will guide your thinking through the specific step; Frequently Asked Questions, which will address the most common questions we heard from our clients; and Key Points, which will reinforce the main elements of the section. You'll also find a place for Notes, where you can record your progress, your frustrations, and even your victories of self-editing.

The Race to the Finish Line

The self-editing process is a lot like running a relay race. First you need to warm-up, line up at the starting line, listen for the crack of the gun, and then run your heart out. While running, you need to complete a certain number of laps before you can hand off the baton and cross the finish line.

An important component of self-editing is that, just like a relay, you can't do it alone. You will need a trusted team member to help you throughout the race so you can cross the finish line with a sense of satisfaction.

Are you ready? Let's get started. Your warm-up begins.

Knowing Your Problems is Half the Battle

"The first draft of anything is shit."
–Ernest Hemingway, American writer

In order to improve your performance, you need to first identify your challenges. This holds true for any skill you're trying to master. For example, if you are a runner and want to improve your 5K race time, you need to know what's slowing you down. So you take stock of the possibilities:

➤ Is your gear up to par?
➤ Do you need a lighter pair of running shoes?
➤ Are you in good physical shape?
➤ Do you need to lose a few pounds?
➤ Do you need better training?

The list of questions can be extensive, depending on your circumstances. To show how important this questioning process is, consider this: If you're running races that are just over three miles up and down hills, and your training runs are only two miles on flat ground, you will certainly struggle on race day. But until you analyze and question your performance, you'll never make the connection and improve your results.

The same thing goes for self-editing. Whether preparing to race or preparing to edit your own work, without first knowing the challenges that lie ahead, you will never be satisfied with your performance.

So for the purposes of self-editing, knowing what to fix means that you first need to identify your writing challenges. For most people, the phrase "identify your writing challenges" brings to mind images of high school English teachers handing back essays with red ink all over them. After scanning for the letter grade and then giving a sigh of relief (or maybe a groan of anguish), most of us didn't even read the comments the teacher wrote. That's too bad, because if we had, our writing might be better today.

The fact is that your writing is a reflection of you. When someone reads your writing, they are left with an impression of you, either favorable or unfavorable. People can make judgments on your creativity, education level, attention to detail, and your subject matter expertise based solely on your writing. So even if you are the utmost expert in your field, all your expertise will appear worthless if your writing is riddled with errors. No matter what type of writing you are doing, you need to put your best foot forward. To do that, you need to evaluate your writing weaknesses and fix them.

Past, Present, and Future

For most of us, our writing challenges are deep rooted. From the time we created our first sentence back in grammar school, we formed the foundation of our writing—challenges and all. As the years went on, we found that we struggled with some of the complexities of the English language, some more than others. And in fact, many of the writing mistakes we made then still haunt us today. Despite the best efforts from our teachers and parents, those writing challenges are still there, years (and years) later.

What makes matters worse is that as adults, we no longer have to worry about letter grades or angry parents. We don't get direct feedback on our writing anymore. The feedback comes via less obvious actions. For example, if our client declines our services after reading our written proposal, we make excuses that the client must have changed his or her needs. If an editor rewrites our article, we think the editor must not understand the topic. If the corporate communications director instructs us to rewrite our press release, we think he or she does not appreciate sales writing. We're always blaming the other person when our writing is not clear.

Fortunately, it's never too late to learn how to write better. Sure, you'll have to invest some time and effort on your part, but the results will be worth it.

The Ground Rules

Step one is to learn about your writing challenges. Here are the ground rules to get you started.

Ground Rule #1:
Evaluate what problems appear repeatedly in your writing.

Once we start making writing errors, they stick with us for a long time. Fortunately, by looking at samples of our past writing we can identify the problems we have today. Look in your file drawer for business writing you've done or dig through boxes of old school papers in your attic. It's okay if they are marked up by a teacher or boss; that will actually be helpful.

Be warned that one of the biggest roadblocks to objectively evaluating your work is your emotional attachment to the piece. Forget about the topic, the time you spent on it, the recognition you received from it, etc. Look at the writing from a purely technical standpoint. As you read through your samples, take notes on the errors you've made. After you complete your notes, look for generalizations in the types of errors. For example, do you commonly misspell words, do you have a problem using commas, or is your writing full of run-on sentences?

☑ Ground Rule #2:
Check if your ideas are organized in the text.

Organization is a frequent challenge. If people read your writing and ask, "What did you mean by this?" then that is a sign your writing isn't organized. Your writing may make perfect sense to you because you're familiar with the subject, but if your ideas aren't organized, someone who reads your writing won't be able to follow what you're saying.

To check if your writing is organized, read each paragraph as a stand-alone unit. In the margin next to each paragraph, write a one- or two-word description of what the paragraph is about. When you're done, read the margin notes you've written. Are keywords and concepts together, and do the keyword concepts flow logically? Could someone look at your notes in the margins and follow a sequence? If not, then your work is not organized.

☑ Ground Rule #3: Look for the topic sentence in the beginning of each paragraph.

A topic sentence is the first sentence in the paragraph and tells the reader the paragraph's subject. All subsequent sentences in the paragraph should relate to the topic sentence. Without it, your writing will be confusing.

For example, you know how annoying it is when drivers change lanes without signaling. When you write a paragraph without a topic sentence, you are doing the same thing. You're jumping from thought to thought (lane to lane) without warning others of your new direction. So read each paragraph and identify the topic sentence. Do all the sentences in the paragraph support the topic sentence? Do your paragraphs even have a topic sentence?

☑ Ground Rule #4:
Scan your writing for repetition.

Nothing is more boring than reading the same word over and over and over. Scan your document to see if you use certain words too often. In a computer document, you can always use the "find" tool in your word processing program to learn exactly how many times you used the repetitive word. If a main word comes up 12 times on one page, chances are you've used it too frequently.

☑ Ground Rule #5:
Ensure that you vary your sentence structure.

Just as eating peanut butter and jelly sandwiches every day would be boring, so would writing the same sentence type over and over. Subject-verb-object sentences are technically okay. However, if it's the only sentence form you use, your writing will sound very choppy and monotonous. Look at the beginning, middle, and end of your sentences. Are they all identical constructions? If so, you may need to investigate new sentence structures to make your writing more interesting. Remember, good writing isn't just about being grammatically correct; it's about engaging your readers with the rhythm and melody of the words.

Ground Rule #6: Go through a grammar guide to answer questions about your specific writing challenges.

Just as each person is unique in personality and behavioral patterns, so too are each person's writing challenges. If you have questions about the specific problems you're identifying, page through a detailed grammar guide and get your specific questions answered. This does not mean you have to memorize the rules. However, once you have an idea of which grammar issues to focus on, you'll be well on your way to successful self-editing.

Some Real-Life Samples

Following are some writing samples and the challenges that were spotted in each. These samples will give you an idea of how to analyze your writing objectively.

Ground Rules in Action

The three writing samples that follow come from three different and distinct writing sectors. One is from a corporate newsletter, one is from web copy, and the last one is from a college student. It just goes to show that every writer has a challenge or two. No one is perfect.

Example #1: Using Margin Notes to Check for Organization of Ideas

The following is an excerpt from an article that was to appear in a company newsletter. While the writing itself is good, the piece's organization needs some help.

Belongs later.
Don't see point
of question yet.

How do you think your sales would increase if your crew sold your customers on Fast Food Company X rather than just selling drinks and burgers?

Real intro to
topic. Move up.

During a recent business trip I met a very dynamic person. This person isn't a celebrity, a motivational speaker, or even a guidance counselor; however she could easily become or do anything she wished. Believe it or not, this dynamic person is an airline stewardess who works endless hours serving ungrateful people drinks and pretzels.

Intro to topic.

Most of the time when I fly, the airline stewardess isn't usually the most pleasant person to deal with. However, Ruby, the airline stewardess I'm talking about, really knows how to exceed anyone's expectations. Ruby excels in her position because she takes her job seriously while having fun at it. For instance, when I asked Ruby how her day was going, she replied that it was great and if it's ever a bad day, she takes it upon herself to make it become great. All I could say was "WOW!!!"

Call to action point.
Need to move down
because we don't
even know much
about Ruby yet.

You can easily implement Ruby's philosophy in your crew. However, the question is, how do you get your crew motivated about their job let alone get them to take responsibility for going the extra mile? Unfortunately, Ruby's philosophy doesn't come in a can that you can spray on your crew and POOF you have a positive, upbeat crew. But with some work and with your involvement you can create your own type of "Ruby" stores.

Ruby takes responsibility for her day by making it the best it can be. Her positive take-charge attitude makes her job fun rather than a dreadful daily grind. By Ruby exceeding my expectations, she sold me on the airline without even knowing it. Her positive philosophy not only created a positive experience, but it also helped sell another ticket for my next trip. . .

Ruby philosophy. Move up.

Here is the revised newsletter article. Notice how it flows much better with the new organization.

During a recent business trip I met a very dynamic person. This person isn't a celebrity, a motivational speaker, or even a guidance counselor; however she could easily become or do anything she wished. Believe it or not, this dynamic person is an airline stewardess who works endless hours serving ungrateful people drinks and pretzels.

Most of the time when I fly, the airline stewardess isn't usually the most pleasant person to deal with. However, Ruby, the airline stewardess I'm talking about, really knows how to exceed anyone's expectations. Ruby excels in her position because she takes her job seriously while having fun at it. For instance, when I asked Ruby how her day was going, she replied that it was great and if it's ever a bad day, she takes it upon herself to make it become great. All I could say was "WOW!!!"

Ruby takes responsibility for her day by making it the best it can be. Her positive take-charge attitude makes her job fun rather than a dreadful daily grind. By Ruby exceeding my expectations, she sold me on the airline without even knowing it. Her positive philosophy not only created a positive experience, but it also helped sell another ticket for my next trip.

How do you think your sales would increase if your crew sold your customers on Fast Food Company X rather than just selling drinks and burgers?

You can easily implement Ruby's philosophy
in your crew. However, the question is, how do
you get your crew motivated about their job let
alone get them to take responsibility for going
the extra mile? Unfortunately, Ruby's philosophy doesn't come in a can that you can spray
on your crew and POOF you have a positive,
upbeat crew. But with some work and with your
involvement you can create your own type of
"Ruby" stores . . .

Example #2: Identifying Topic Sentences

The following is web copy a company wrote. The company has great ideas, but their paragraph structure made their ideas hard to understand.

Here are some of the benefits of XYZ service. They're amazing. In fact, every internet marketer needs this service. PERIOD! And now you can earn substantial profits providing it. You can build your business with no additional work on your part. Try it. You'll be glad you did.

Topic sentence states, "Here are some of the benefits..." but the paragraph never lists any.

With the XYZ service, internet marketers can automatically email up to seven customized follow-up letters to their prospects over a pre-set period of time. This service will dramatically increase closings and could easily double or triple sales of your products and services. Just imagine implementing this follow-up system! Do you think your commission check would grow? Plus you could receive thousands of dollars in commissions from XYZ Company on a monthly basis for promoting this service. This program works best when promoted vigorously; however, many webmasters earn substantial income through passive promotion by simply placing a link on their web site. To get started immediately go to http://www.com

Topic sentence tells a feature of the service, but the rest of the paragraph does not explain the feature. In fact, it goes off onto another topic.

Since this web copy had faulty or missing topic sentences, we had to rewrite the paragraphs so they better focus on the necessary elements. Notice how the paragraphs now guide you through the thought process, from topic sentence to paragraph completion.

The benefits of XYZ service will enable you to earn substantial profits so you can build your business with no additional work on your part. In fact, every internet marketer who is serious about his or her business needs this service and the many benefits it offers. Try it. You'll be glad you did.

With the XYZ service, internet marketers can automatically email up to seven customized follow-up letters to their prospects over a pre-set period of time. This service will enable you to dramatically increase closings and could easily double or triple sales of your products and services.

By implementing this follow-up system, your commission check can quickly grow. Plus you could receive thousands of dollars in commissions from XYZ Company on a monthly basis for promoting this service. This program works best when promoted vigorously; however, many webmasters earn substantial income through passive promotion by simply placing a link on their web site. To get started immediately go to http://www.com

Example #3: Identifying Repetition

Repetition can take on many forms. Some writers use repetition when they use two words where one will do. Others add useless modifiers (i.e.: completely finished). And some use added surplus intensifiers (i.e.: purple in color). The author of the following paragraph was a college student in a creative writing class. Notice how we re-wrote the paragraph to eliminate the wordiness.

Wordy version (74 words):

Wordy

Anne was an absolutely typical kind of University freshman. Although her mind was actually full of the kind of information she could use as the basis for a research paper, she was sure and certain that she had nothing to write about. And by this point in time, she thought her situation was totally hopeless. She could only hope and trust that some wonderful miracle would come along to rescue her from terrible disaster.

"sure" and "certain" mean the same thing

Wordy

Useless modifier- aren't all disasters terrible?

Revised version (57 words):

Anne was a typical University freshman. Although her mind was full of information she could use as the basis for a research paper, she was sure she had nothing to write about. And by this time, she thought the situation was hopeless. She could only hope that some miracle would come along to rescue her from disaster.

The leaner, revised version tells the same story, but with fewer words. And because the text is less wordy, it actually reads better and is more coherent.

Test Yourself

Still can't quite figure out what you need to include on your self-editing checklist? Below are several sentences. Each contains a writing challenge or two. Go through each of the following sentences and identify the error. At the end, you can see how many of each type you got wrong. Add those challenges to your checklist.

Note: Every sentence has something incorrect with it. In the space provided write down what needs to be corrected.

➢ 1. It is time consuming to conduct research on the internet.

_____

_____

➢ 2. Each of the employees got their own coffee.

_____

_____

➢ 3. I seperated the data into three different worksheets.

_____

_____

➢ 4. For the meeting, I was told to bring the following; a whiteboard, markers, a laptop, and my sense of humor.

_____

_____

➢ 5. Though John really thought he had his act together he soon found that he hadn't planned for a dip in sales and his company went bankrupt and then he had to find a new job.

_____

_____

_____

_____

➤ 6. With her unexpected day off, Lisa couldn't decide whether to repaint her apartment, laying out at the pool, or goof off.

_____

_____

_____

➤ 7. She didn't not lock her door.

_____

_____

➤ 8. Callie enjoys ballet class, and she dances so good.

_____

_____

➤ 9. As long as I have known her she has had long hair.

_____

_____

➤ 10. Too many abreviations make sentences difficult to read.

_____

_____

➤ 11. The contest was won by the girl in the red dress.

_____

_____

➤ 12. She always wanted to have a baby; a little girl who looked just like daddy.

_____

_____

➤ 13. Leaving the house, the door was unlocked.

_____

_____

➢ 14. The group of boys are getting loud.

_____

_____

➢ 15. Jake enjoyed soccer, practicing the violin, and cheeseburgers.

_____

_____

➢ 16. Please except me for who I am.

_____

_____

➢ 17. It is getting difficult to effectively manage my time.

_____

_____

➢ 18. That ain't no way to treat a lady.

_____

_____

➢ 19. Addressing the audience Senator Black suggested a bill
be passed to lower health insurance and that was not well
received by the audience.

_____

_____

_____

➢ 20. The box, which had four sides and a lid, closed tightly.

_____

_____

➢ 21. Meet me at the capital building.

_____

_____

➢ 22. The girl swatted at the bee in the pink dress.

_____

➢ 23. "Please get down, John said Melissa.

_____

➢ 24. I went to the store to get the standard pre-snowstorm items, bread, milk, eggs, and toilet paper.

_____

_____

➢ 25. The food which I bought from the farmer's market was quite fresh.

_____

_____

➢ 26. The challenge of self-editing is the biggest challenge when it comes to writing well.

_____

_____

➢ 27. The boy gave me a smile every day but always wants me to give him candy.

_____

_____

➢ 28. The accountant over there-the one with the clipboard and dark-rimmed glasses-is going to do my taxes this year.

_____

_____

➢ 29. Don't chew with your mouth open, it's not polite.

_____

➢ 30. During the last 5 years, $50,000 of debt was incurred by the young couple.

_____

_____

How Did You Do?

➢   **1. Incorrect**: It is time consuming to conduct research on the Internet.

☑   **1. Correct**: Conducting Internet research is time consuming.

Problem: *Wordiness.* The original sentence contains ten words, while the new sentence contains six. Additionally, the revised sentence is more engaging.

➢   **2. Incorrect**: Each of the employees got their own coffee.

☑   **2. Correct**: Each of the employees got her own coffee.

Problem: *Subject/verb agreement.* The subject "each" is singular, but "their" is plural.

➢   **3. Incorrect**: I seperated the data into three different worksheets.

☑   **3. Correct**: I separated the data into three different worksheets.

Problem: *Spelling.* "Separated" is misspelled.

➢   **4. Incorrect**: For the meeting, I was told to bring the following; a whiteboard, markers, a laptop, and my sense of humor.

☑   **4. Correct**: For the meeting, I was told to bring the following: a whiteboard, markers, a laptop, and my sense of humor.

Problem: *Punctuation.* Before lists, use a colon, not a semicolon.

➤ **5. Incorrect**: Though John really thought he had his act together he soon found that he hadn't planned for a dip in sales and his company went bankrupt and then he had to find a new job.

☑ **5. Correct**: Though John really thought he had his act together, he soon found that he hadn't planned for a dip in sales. His company went bankrupt, and then he had to find a new job.

Problem: *Run-on sentence.* The original sentence has too many ideas in it to be one thought.

➤ **6. Incorrect:** With her unexpected day off, Lisa couldn't decide whether to repaint her apartment, laying out at the pool, or goof off.

☑ **6. Correct:** With her unexpected day off, Lisa couldn't decide whether to repaint her apartment, lay out at the pool, or goof off.

Problem: *Parallelism.* All three of Lisa's options must be parallel in construction.

➤ **7. Incorrect:** She didn't not lock her door.

☑ **7. Corect:** She locked her door.

Problem: *Double negative.* The original sentence is too confusing.

➤ **8. Incorrect:** Callie enjoys ballet class, and she dances so good.

☑ **8. Correct:** Callie enjoys ballet class, and she dances so well.

Problem: *Confusing adverbs and adjectives.* Callie is a "good dancer" (adjective), but she "dances well" (adverb).

➤ **9. Incorrect:** As long as I have known her she has had long hair.

☑ **9. Correct:** As long as I have known her, she has had long hair.

Problem: *Punctuation.* Insert a comma after "her."

➤ **10. Incorrect:** Too many abreviations make sentences difficult to read.

☑ **10. Correct:** Too many abbreviations make sentences difficult to read.

Problem: *Spelling error.* "Abbreviations" is misspelled.

➤ **11. Incorrect:** The contest was won by the girl in the red dress.

☑ **11. Correct:** The girl in the red dress won the contest.

Problem: *Passive sentence.* The noun must do the verb's action.

➤ **12. Incorrect:** She always wanted to have a baby; a little girl who looked just like daddy.

☑ **12. Correct:** She always wanted to have a baby: a little girl who looked just like daddy.

Problem: *Punctuation.* Use a colon to indicate that a description of the previous thought is following.

➤ **13. Incorrect:** Leaving the house, the door was un-locked.

☑ **13. Correct:** Leaving the house, I left the door un-locked.

Problem: *Dangling modifier.* In the first sentence, it reads that the door left the house. The phrase "leaving the house" is not modify-ing the person or thing that left the house.

➢ **14. Incorrect:** The group of boys are getting loud.

☑ **14. Correct:** The group of boys is getting loud.

Problem: *Subject/verb agreement.* The word "group" needs a singular verb.

➢ **15. Incorrect**: Jake enjoyed soccer, practicing the violin, and cheeseburgers.

☑ **15. Correct:** Jake enjoyed playing soccer, practicing the violin, and eating cheeseburgers.

Problem: *Parallelism.* Jake's activities must be in parallel construction.

➢ **16. Incorrect:** Please except me for who I am.

☑ **16. Correct:** Please accept me for who I am.

Problem: *Homonym confusion.* Except versus accept.

➢ **17. Incorrect:** It is getting difficult and hard to effectively manage my time.

☑ **17. Correct:** Effectively managing my time is getting difficult.

Problem: *Wordiness.* The original sentence has eleven words, while the revised sentence has seven words.

➢ **18. Incorrect:** That ain't no way to treat a lady.

☑ **18. Correct:** That is no way to treat a lady.

Problem: *Double negative.* Double negatives are confusing to readers.

➢ **19. Incorrect:** Addressing the audience, Senator Black suggested a bill be passed to lower health insurance and that was not well received by the audience.

☑ **19. Correct:** Addressing the audience, Senator Black suggested a bill be passed to lower health insurance. The audience did not receive the suggestion well.

Problem: *Run-on sentence and passive sentence construction.* Break up the two thoughts in the sentence, and rewrite the second one so it's not passive.

➢ **20. Incorrect:** The square box, which had four sides and a lid, closed tightly.

☑ **20. Correct:** The square box closed tightly.

Problem: *Redundancy.* Don't all square boxes have four sides and a lid?

➢ **21. Incorrect:** Meet me at the capital building.

☑ **21. Correct:** Meet me at the capitol building.

Problem: *Homonym confusion.* Capital versus capitol.

➢ **22. Incorrect:** The girl swatted at the bee in the pink dress.

☑ **22. Correct:** The girl in the pink dress swatted at the bee.

Problem: *Misplaced modifier.* The original sentence reads as if the bee is wearing the pink dress.

➢ **23. Incorrect:** "Please get down, John said Melissa.

☑ **23. Correct:** "Please get down, John" said Melissa.

Problem: *Punctuation.* Missing quotation marks.

➤ **24. Incorrect:** I went to the store to get the standard pre-snowstorm items, bread, milk, eggs, and toilet paper.

☑ **24. Correct**: I went to the store to get the standard pre-snowstorm items: bread, milk, eggs, and toilet paper.

Problem: *Punctuation.* Use a colon to indicate a list of things.

➤ **25. Incorrect:** The food which I bought from the farmer's market was quite fresh.

☑ **25. Correct:** The food that I bought from the farmer's market was quite fresh.

Problem: *Use of "which" versus "that."* The original sentence construction suggests that the phrase "which I bought from the farmer's market" is needed for the sentence's comprehension (a restrictive clause). Therefore, use "that" for a restrictive clause, and "which" for a non-restrictive clause.

➤ **26. Incorrect:** The challenge of self-editing is the biggest challenge when it comes to writing well.

☑ **26. Correct:** The challenge of self-editing is the biggest obstacle when it comes to writing well.

Problem: *Word repetition.* In the original sentence, the word "challenge" appears twice.

➤ **27. Incorrect:** The boy gave me a smile every day but always wants me to give him candy.

☑ **27. Correct:** Te boy gave me a smile every day but always wanted me to give him candy.

Problem: *Tense shift.* "Gave" is past tense, while "wants" is present tense. Keep your tenses consistent.

➤ **28. Incorrect:** The accountant over there-the one with the clipboard and dark-rimmed glasses-is going to do my taxes this year.

☑ **28. Correct**: The accountant over there—the one with the clipboard and dark-rimmed glasses—is going to do my taxes this year.

Problem: *Punctuation.* Use a hyphen instead of a dash.

☑ **29. Incorrect:** Don't chew with your mouth open, it's not polite.

☑ **29. Correct:** Don't chew with your mouth open; it's not polite.

Problem: *Punctuation.* When you join two thoughts with a comma, you've create a comma spliced sentence. Replace the comma with a semicolon, or break it up into two separate sentences.

➤ **30. Incorrect:** During the last 5 years, $50,000 of debt was incurred by the young couple.

☑ **30. Correct:** The young couple incurred $50,000 of debt during the last 5 years.

Problem: *Passive sentence.* Make sure the noun is doing the verb's action.

Scoring

Look back at which sentences you got wrong. Then look at the corresponding challenge. You may want to add these challenges to your editing checklist.

Challenge	Question Number
Wordiness	1, 17
Subject Verb Agreement	2, 14
Spelling	3, 10
Punctuation	4, 9, 12, 23, 28, 29
Run-On Sentence	5, 19
Parallelism	6, 15
Double Negative	7, 18
Adverb versus Adjective Use	8
Passive Sentence	11, 19, 30
Dangling or Misplaced Modifier	12, 22
Homonym Confusion	16, 21
Redundancy or Repetition	20, 26
That versus Which Use	25
Tense Shift	27

Frequently Asked Questions

Q. The creativity I have with my writing is my strength. Why can't I just let my editor continue to fix my technical mistakes?

A. Well, you can, but you're never going to improve your writing that way. Plus, your editor may eventually get tired of fixing the same issues in your writing each time, or he or she may simply stop editing in general for other reasons (retirement, illness, career change, etc.) Then you'll be stuck trying to find a new editor who you feel comfortable working with. If your editor works for a book or magazine publisher, realize that his or her job is not to rewrite your work. Editors expect you to turn in well-written text (you are, after all, the writer). Their job is simply to enhance it. If you work in a corporate setting, your lack of self-editing may prevent you from being promoted. For example, if you can't write an effective sales letter, how can you manage a group of salespeople and expect them to write effective letters? Finally, your writing will come easier to you once you have mastered more of the basic mechanics.

Q. I just can't seem to be objective about the weaknesses of my writing. What can I do?

A. This is a fairly common problem. One option is to ask someone you know who is a good writer to review your work. You could ask a friend, a co-worker, an executive assistant, etc. But be careful with this option, because if your writing isn't that strong to begin with, can you really judge whether someone else's writing is correct? Depending on your skill level, a better option may be to hire a professional editor to review your work. If money is an issue, you could check with your local college. Many junior or senior level English majors would welcome a few extra bucks to evaluate your writing.

Q. Why do I have to worry about grammar, spelling, and sentence structure? Isn't that what my spell and grammar check are for?

A. Even though spelling and grammar check can be useful tools, you can't hit "change" each time it flags a problem. It may not recognize some words you are using, especially names or industry-specific terms.

It also may tell you your grammar or sentence structure is wrong, when it really isn't. View this "tool" as just that. Pay close attention each time the tool identifies a potential problem to determine who is right—you or the computer. If you don't know the reasoning behind why the potential problem was flagged, you won't know whether it's really wrong.

Key Points

➤ You can overcome your writing challenges.

➤ You will need to analyze your past writing to improve your future writing.

➤ Fixing your writing requires concerted effort on your part.

➤ Good writing goes beyond basic mechanics and grammar.

➤ Self-editing is a valuable skill that, once mastered, will positively impact your future.

Turning Points –
Questions for Self-Reflection

Your answers to these questions will help you plan your self-editing process.

➤ Some phrases about my writing that I hear from co-workers, clients, or friends include:

_____

_____

_____

_____

_____

_____

_____

_____

_____

_____

_____

_____

_____

_____

_____

_____

_____

➤   From this feedback I get the impression that my writing is:

_____

_____

_____

_____

_____

_____

_____

_____

_____

_____

_____

_____

_____

_____

_____

_____

_____

_____

➢ I want to improve my self-editing skills because:

_____

_____

_____

_____

_____

_____

_____

_____

_____

_____

_____

_____

_____

_____

_____

_____

_____

_____

Preparation Makes Perfect

"Write quickly and you will never write well. Write well, and you will soon write quickly."

–Fabius Quintilianus, 65 A.D., Roman Rhetorician

Now that you know what your challenges are, you need to "warm up" your editing muscle. Just as you can't immediately go from touching your toes to running at breakneck speed, neither can you transition that quickly from knowing your writing challenges to editing. You need to stretch, get your blood pumping, and visualize yourself running the race in perfect form.

Solid preparation is vital at this stage. Think about it...don't you prepare for everything else you do in life? Don't you prepare for tests, prepare for your vacation, prepare for job interviews, prepare for big meetings, prepare for the holidays...you get the picture. Preparation helps you yield better results in so many other aspects of life; self-editing is no different.

Additionally, studies have shown that those people who prepare for an endeavor have a higher chance of meeting the goals they've outlined for themselves. So if one of your goals is to better self-edit your work, then you definitely need to prepare. Only then will you have the final product you know is possible.

Think Like an Editor, not a Writer

Some people mistakenly believe that preparation is one of those "time wasting" activities. They think that because they're not doing a task directly related to what they want to accomplish (they're not marking a paper with red ink), they're not doing anything "productive." Thinking actually is productive. In fact, some of our most brilliant ideas and advanced techniques come when we're in a planning and preparation phase.

Now, preparation is not all about laying the foundation. A big part of preparation is mindset. So during this phase of the process, you're not only building the foundation on which to edit, but you're also making sure you're mentally ready for the task. Without your mind ready to take action, you won't have good results.

"But of course I want to self-edit," you may be thinking. "That's why I'm reading this book." And on the surface that may true. Realize though that some mental blocks you have against editing or even some poor editing habits can be holding you back from truly editing like a pro. Only when you change your mindset to that of an editor rather than a writer, and do the things that editors do, can you self-edit effectively.

So, what's the difference between an editor's mindset and a writer's mindset? Good question. Writers tend to be very attached to their work. And this is understandable. They did, after all, spend a great deal of time creating their "baby." But this attachment is also their downfall when it comes to self-editing. They are often so attached that they can't look at their work objectively.

Editors, on the other hand, are objective. They aren't attached to any word or idea on the page. They know the goal is to express a point in an accurate and compelling way, regardless of the writer's feelings. So if the piece doesn't read well, the editor has no issues revising it. The editor doesn't care if it took five hours to create that perfect sentence. If that sentence has no business being there, the editor will delete it.

So while you certainly do want to love your written work and be passionate about it, you also need to balance that passion with objectivity. Yes, the passion is what motivates you to write in the first place, but it's the objectivity that will free you to edit the piece so it's good enough to be worthy of your passion.

The Ground Rules

Step two of self-editing is to make all the necessary preparations so you can begin to edit. Here are the ground rules to get you organized.

☑ **Ground Rule #1:**
Build a personalized editing checklist.

Once you've identified your error patterns (see Step One), you need to create a personalized editing checklist. To do this, take a piece of paper and list all your writing challenges. Rank them in descending order of frequency. For example, if 55% of your writing errors involve switching back and forth between tenses, list that one first; if 25% of your errors involve spelling, list that second; if 20% of your writing errors involve writing passive sentence, list that third, and so on. Save your list. When you self-edit, have this list handy so you can focus on each problem area during the editing process. Eventually, having your list in front of you when you write will allow you to conquer your challenges while writing, and save you time in the editing process.

☑ **Ground Rule #2:**
Schedule time for the editing phase.

The single biggest mistake writers make is that they don't schedule time for the editing process. They feel their job is to write and their editor's job is to "clean up their mess." That's not true. An editor's job is to enhance your writing and make it sound better, not rewrite your piece. As a writer, you should always strive to have your writing as polished as possible before it even reaches your editor's hands.

Think of it this way: When a computer programmer writes code, he or she revises that code until it's perfect (or as close to perfect as the programmer can get it). The programmer then gives the newly coded program to a product tester, whose job is to test the program code. The tester's job is not to rewrite the code. The tester's job is to see if the code works and if the program performs the way a user would want it to. The tester will give the programmer some input and suggestions on how to make the program code more effective, but that's it. It's the same with writers and editors. The writer writes the text, and the editor helps make it better.

This means some extra work for you, but your effort will pay off in the long run. The general rule of thumb is to plan for half the time you spend writing a piece to edit it. In other words, if it takes you six hours to write a piece, schedule three hours to edit it. If time allows, plan your editing session for the day after you've finished writing. This gives your writing a chance to "cool." You'll have fresh eyes and more objectivity.

☑ Ground Rule #3:
Detach from the work.

If you're too attached to your work, you'll never edit it effectively. You'll hang onto every idea and sentence in your piece because you worked so hard to create it. However, when you detach from your text, you can see it objectively, like an editor. For some writers, detaching from their text is simply a matter of time. That is, they need to leave the piece for a day or two before they can let go of the emotion of writing it. Other writers detach by physically changing their location when they edit. So rather than edit the work in the place where they wrote it (in their office, for example), they do their editing at the kitchen table or in the company conference room. Still, the more advanced writers are simply able to shift their mindset to that of an editor and let go of the work. They've reconciled within themselves that their masterpiece does need some tweaking, and they're willing to revise it as necessary.

☑ Ground Rule #4:
Work on a hard-copy.

Reading text on a computer screen is tough on your eyes. When your eyes are tired, you easily miss even the most obvious grammar errors and typos. Print out your document on fresh white paper. Take that hard copy and go anywhere other than your office or where you wrote the piece. Remember, too, that while in front of your computer, you will have the mindset of a writer. Additionally, most people find that actually holding their words in their hands makes them feel like an editor instead of a writer. Since the keyboard is nowhere in sight, your brain realizes the writing phase is over, and it's time to fine-tune.

Some Real-Life Samples

Following are some sample editing checklists and a sample schedule to show you how easy this part of the process is.

Ground Rules in Action

The two editing checklists that follow come from two different types of people. One is an author by profession, and the other is a "money" person who chose a non-writing related field on purpose. Notice how each checklist is customized to the person's main writing challenges.

Example #1: Editing Checklists

Anne: A professional speaker and author

Anne needed to strengthen her writing and enhance her self-editing skills so she could write handouts and workbooks to go along with her workshops.

Anne's Editing Checklist:

➤ Challenge #1: Organization (45%) – Keep the material logical so my workshop participants can follow along.

➤ Challenge #2: Passive sentence construction (30%) – Keep my writing active so my workshop participants are engaged.

➤ Challenge #3: Spelling (10%) – Slow down and really check my spelling. Sometimes my fingers don't type as fast as my brain thinks, and I make silly spelling errors.

➤ Challenge #4: Fragment sentences (10%) – Remember that speaking and writing are two different mediums. Sometimes I forget that I can't write the way I speak.

➤ Challenge #5: Transitions (5%) – Move from thought to thought smoothly by adding transitions. Without transitions my writing sounds jumpy.

Richard: A Financial Planner

Richard needed to strengthen his writing and enhance his self-editing skills so he could better prospect for new business and keep in touch with his current clients.

Richard's Editing Checklist

➤ Challenge #1: Passive sentence construction (50%) – In business school we learned to write in passive voice. Clients find that boring. Keep my writing active so people actually read my letters.

➤ Challenge #2: Wordiness (30%) – Write what I want in as few words as possible. Clients don't want to be impressed with my big sentences. They want to understand complex financial information. Continually ask myself, "Do I really need that word or phrase?"

➤ Challenge #3: Redundant sentence structures (10%) – Vary my sentence structure so my letters are more interesting to read.

➤ Challenge #4: Possessive nouns (5%) – I often get possessive and plural mixed up. Look to see if the noun or pronoun in the sentence is showing ownership.

➤ Challenge #5: Semicolons (5%) – A semicolon is a stronger pause than a comma, but a weaker pause than a period. Use a semicolon to join related ideas.

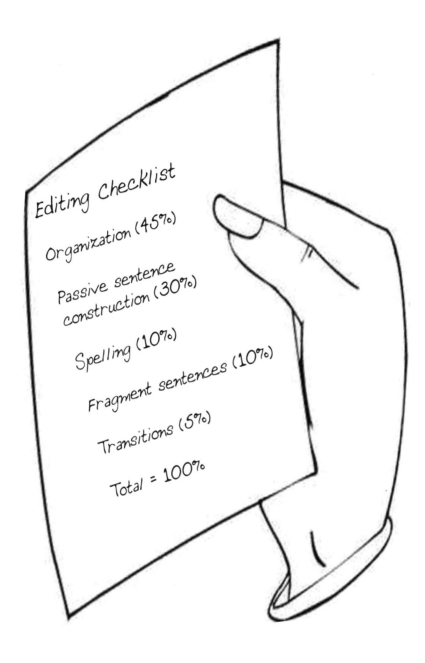

Editing Checklist

Organization (45%)

Passive sentence
construction (30%)

Spelling (10%)

Fragment sentences (10%)

Transitions (5%)

Total = 100%

Keep a list such as this to remind yourself
of your writing challenges.

Example #2: Sample Schedule

Think you can't find time to self-edit your work? Think again.
Look how this busy professional was able to fit in the necessary
editing time. This is Richard's schedule. He needed to find four
hours to edit a new prospect information kit that took him eight
hours to create.

- ➢ 5 a.m. to 6 a.m. – Edit info kit (1 hour). [Note: Richard woke
  an hour early to fit this time in.]

- ➢ 6 a.m. to 7 a.m. – Shower and get ready for day.

- ➢ 7 a.m. to 7:30 a.m. – Wake kids and help get them dressed.

- ➢ 7:30 a.m. to 8 a.m. – Breakfast with kids.

- ➢ 8 a.m. to 8:30 a.m. – Drop kids off at school and drive to
  office.

- ➢ 8:30 a.m. to 9 a.m. – Review info kit while computer and
  other office equipment starts up (1/2 hour). [Note: Richard
  decided to forgo his usual coffee meeting with some colleagues to fit this time in.]

- ➢ 9 a.m. to 10:30 a.m. – Client business.

- ➢ 10:30 a.m. to 11:30 a.m. – Scheduled info kit editing time
  (1 hour). [Note: This was the only time Richard officially
  scheduled in his day planner.]

- ➢ 11:30 a.m. to 12:30 p.m. – Client business.

- ➢ 12:30 p.m. to 1:30 p.m. – Lunch break. Edit info kit (1
  hour). [Note: Richard decided to eat lunch at his desk while
  he looked over the info kit rather than go out with co-workers.]

- ➢ 1:30 p.m. to 5:30 p.m. – Client business.

- ➢ 5:30 p.m. to 6 p.m. – Drive home.

- ➢ 6 p.m. to 8 p.m. – Evening time with family.

- ➢ 8 p.m. to 8:30 p.m. – Edit info kit (1/2 hour). [Note: Richard
  decided not to watch one of his favorite television programs
  to fit this time in.]

By using his time wisely and making some conscious decisions about his priorities, Richard was able to fit four hours of editing time into his hectic schedule.

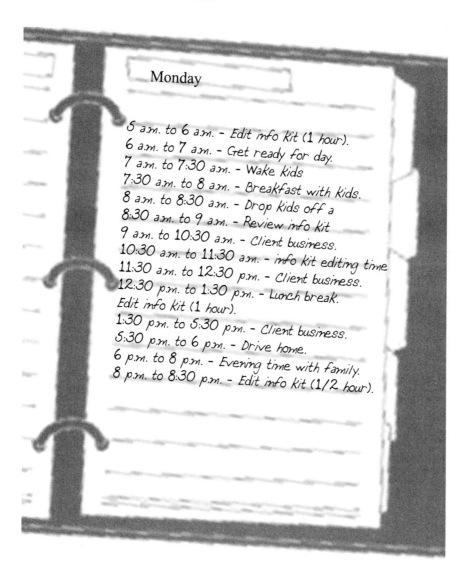

Monday

5 a.m. to 6 a.m. - Edit info kit (1 hour).
6 a.m. to 7 a.m. - Get ready for day.
7 a.m. to 7:30 a.m. - Wake kids
7:30 a.m. to 8 a.m. - Breakfast with kids.
8 a.m. to 8:30 a.m. - Drop kids off a
8:30 a.m. to 9 a.m. - Review info kit
9 a.m. to 10:30 a.m. - Client business.
10:30 a.m. to 11:30 a.m. - info kit editing time
11:30 a.m. to 12:30 p.m. - Client business.
12:30 p.m. to 1:30 p.m. - Lunch break.
Edit info kit (1 hour).
1:30 p.m. to 5:30 p.m. - Client business.
5:30 p.m. to 6 p.m. - Drive home.
6 p.m. to 8 p.m. - Evening time with family.
8 p.m. to 8:30 p.m. - Edit info kit (1/2 hour).

Schedule your editing time in your planner.
Yes; it's that important.

Frequently Asked Questions

Q: Sometimes I think my writing is perfect when I hand it over to my editor, but then when it comes back to me, I'm embarrassed by the obvious flaws I missed. How can I prevent this in the future?

A: You may not have a "fresh eye" when you're editing. Make sure you give your piece a chance to "cool." You often won't find all the mistakes if you edit the day of your writing. Here's an experiment for you to try: Do your writing and editing on the same day until you're confident your piece is finished. Then put the piece aside for a day. Take it out the next morning and reread it. You'll likely see many opportunities to improve your "perfect" piece.

Q: Isn't printing out a hard copy for editing a waste of printer ink and paper? What if I darken my computer monitor settings so it's easier on my eyes? Would it be okay to edit on-screen then?

A: Sure, you could darken your screen and try editing that way. But you'll still miss plenty of things. No matter how dark or big you make the text on your computer screen, you are really much better off printing out your work on a hard copy. For one thing, it's portable so you can read it somewhere else where you are more comfortable and objective. Additionally, when you actually begin editing, you will be able to make notes and corrections on the paper with a pen. You will be able to distinguish between what you originally wrote and the changes you made more easily than if you did it on screen.

Q. I'm too busy to devote this much time to editing. Can't I just hire this part of the process out?

A. Yes. You can hire freelance editors and editorial firms to help you edit your work. This is a viable alternative for many writers and business professionals who are short on time. However, you still need to learn the self-editing process for yourself. Always relying on an outsider to edit your work can add even more time to a project than if you did the editing yourself. Additionally, if you always let someone else edit for you, you'll never develop the confidence in your writing that you need for future success. So use a fee-based editing service as you deem fit, but also know and practice the editing process yourself so you can grow as a writer and advance in your career.

Key Points

➤ Preparation is a productive action step.

➤ The more you prepare for editing, the easier it will be.

➤ Think like a writer when you're writing, and like an editor when you're self-editing.

➤ Let your objectivity keep your passion in check.

➤ No matter how packed your schedule is, you can always find time to self-edit your work.

Turning Points –
Questions for Self-Reflection

Your answers to these questions will help you plan your self-editing process.

➤ The top five writing challenges I have are:

_____

_____

_____

_____

_____

_____

_____

_____

_____

_____

_____

_____

_____

_____

_____

_____

➤ I can find or make free time for the editing process in my schedule by doing the following:

_____

_____

_____

_____

_____

_____

_____

_____

_____

_____

_____

_____

_____

_____

_____

_____

_____

_____

_____

➢   Some ways I can detach from my work include:

_____

_____

_____

_____

_____

_____

_____

_____

_____

_____

_____

_____

_____

_____

_____

_____

_____

_____

➢ I can get out of my writer's mindset and think like an editor by doing the following:

_____

_____

_____

_____

_____

_____

_____

_____

_____

_____

_____

_____

_____

_____

_____

_____

_____

_____

Going for the Long Haul

"The beautiful part of writing is that you don't have to get it right the first time, unlike, say, a brain surgeon."
–Robert Cormier, American Novelist

Congratulations! You have laid the groundwork for your race. You're now ready to embark on the first leg of your run.

You know why you're not running fast enough and what you need to do to improve your performance. You've done your warm-up. You're now lined up at the starting line, waiting to hear the crack of the gun.

You're mentally prepared to run the race and feeling confident in your abilities. Since you're running a relay, before you can hand the baton off to your running partner, you need to do several laps yourself. You're the first on your team to run, so you need to set a good pace.

As you begin the actual editing process, be aware that this is not a quick sprint. In fact, focusing on speed, rather than results and accuracy, can cause you to overlook many mistakes. Just as a runner needs focused attention to reach the finish line, so do you.

With all this in mind, you will still miss some writing errors, many of which will be very obvious. But this is okay. In fact, think about all the professionally produced books, articles, reports, and brochures you've read over the past year. You likely found many small mistakes in these documents, even though numerous professionals read and approved them before they went to press. Most documents, whether written by an amateur or a professional, have an average of three errors for every 10,000 keystrokes. Keystrokes include every typed letter, punctuation mark, space, and hard return. So take the pressure off yourself to be perfect.

This is why a partner is so important. He or she can help you catch those mistakes you miss. But before you hand your work off to someone else, you will need to do many read throughs until you are absolutely positive your writing is almost flawless.

While this process can be lengthy, don't get discouraged. We've broken it down into small, manageable steps. You'll find it's much easier to tackle one challenge at a time rather than all your challenges at once.

Set the Course for Success

As you begin the actual hands-on editing process, you need to put yourself in the correct mindset. In the last step you needed to switch from a writer's mindset to an editor's mindset. In this step you need to go a bit further.

In addition to having an editor's objectivity, you need to clear your surroundings and your mind of distractions so you can focus on the task at hand. Depending on how you work best, you may need to turn off the radio and television to have complete quiet. Others may need some soothing music in the background to help the mind relax. If you're in an office environment, you may need to close your office door, forward your phone to voicemail, and disable your e-mail notification pop-up.

Also, be sure you're embarking on the editing process during your peak performance hours. In other words, if you're usually sluggish midday, then schedule your editing time for the early morning when you're more awake and focused.

The more you're able to focus, the better your editing experience will be. Focus gives you clarity and enables you to envision a successful outcome. Just as a marathon runner envisions him or herself crossing the finish line to victory, you need to envision yourself succeeding at your editing experience. Additionally, the actual editing process you're about to begin requires concentration. It's much easier for a relaxed brain to concentrate than a stressed one.

So if you've been following the Ground Rules this far, you've blocked off enough time in your schedule to do this step of the process justice. Remember, if it took you six hours to write your piece, you need to plan three hours for editing. Get out your list of writing challenges and keep it right next to you.

On your mark, get set, go! The gun has gone off. It's time to begin.

The Ground Rules

The hands-on editing begins right now. The following ground rules will help you tackle the process logically and efficiently, leaving you with writing that is flawless (or pretty darn close).

☑ **Ground Rule #1:**
Enjoy the first read through.

The first time you read your text, don't actively hunt for writing problems. Read it for enjoyment only. After all, you spent so much time writing the piece that you deserve to sit back and enjoy reading the fruits of your labor. Of course, if you notice a glaring error you can make note of it, but don't specifically look for mistakes. In addition to giving you some enjoyment, this initial, casual read through will help relax your mind so you can focus better later.

☑ **Ground Rule # 2:**
Use your voice for the second read through.

For the second read through, read the piece out loud so you can hear it as well as see it. As you read it out loud, really listen to the words you're saying. Does your tongue stumble over a block of words? Do certain phrases sound funny or out of place? Is a sentence so long that you're gasping for breath by the time you reach the period? Do your own words put you to sleep? All these are signs that a section of your document needs some tweaking.

When you read a document to yourself, you're relying on only your eyes to catch writing errors. However, when you read a document out loud, you're activating your sense of hearing and forcing your brain to concentrate on each individual word rather than visual cluster. Now you not only see missing commas, incorrect words, or subject-verb disagreements, but you can also hear when something sounds out of place. When you hear as well as see what you're writing, you can catch more errors and produce a written document that holds the reader's attention.

☑ **Ground Rule #3:**
   Concentrate on one lap at a time.

Now it's time to refer to your list of writing challenges. You will need to do one read through for each of your writing challenges. So if you have 20 challenges on your list, you'll do a minimum of 20 more read throughs. If you were to read the whole document and try to find every single item on your list in one read through—every subject-verb agreement, every passive sentence, every misspelled word, etc.—you'd be overwhelmed. However, if you are looking for something specific, you will have an easier time finding it. So yes, this step will take some time, especially if you have a long list of writing challenges, but that's why you need to budget at least half the time you spend writing on editing.

As you do each read through, look for one specific thing. For example, if subject-verb agreement is your main issue, then go through the text looking at every subject and verb to make sure they are consistent. Then if challenge number two is passive sentences, you will go through the document looking just for that. And so on.

☑ **Ground Rule #4:**
   Read through from back to front.

If you tend to miss one of your challenges frequently, try to fool your brain by reading out of order. Isolate one sentence at a time, from anywhere in the text, and read that sentence only for grammar issues. Be sure you read only one sentence and not a whole paragraph. After so many readings, your brain memorizes chunks of text. However, when you read a sentence at random, your brain has no surrounding text for it to trigger that memorization. Your brain won't remember where in the text the sentence is and it won't pull up the memorized version; it will actually have to look carefully at that particular sentence, making it easier for you to catch errors.

☑ **Ground Rule #5:**
   When in doubt, use your dictionary or thesaurus to help you make accurate and varied word choices.

When you need to choose a better word, know if you're using the right word, or check spelling, consult your at-home library. If you don't have a dictionary and thesaurus, buy one of each! If you do have a copy, analyze those resources. Are they still up-to-date? Are they easy to use? If not, you may need to invest in some new ones. A dictionary and thesaurus will give you access to spelling, shades of meaning, synonyms, and antonyms. If you're away from your office and need immediate access to these resources, you can always go online. You will find a wide variety of free and fee-based dictionary/thesaurus sites.

The Hand Off

By now you have completed countless read throughs of your work. You've read it aloud, you've checked off every item on your writing challenge checklist, and you've consulted your dictionary and thesaurus when necessary. With all this work behind you, you'll be tempted to hand over your writing to your editor, your department head, or your client.

Not so fast.

While you've had a strong finish to this leg of the race, you haven't yet handed off the baton. You'll find in Step Four how bringing a friend into the editing process can strengthen your writing that much more.

 ## Frequently Asked Questions

Q: It seems like this process is really time-consuming! Can't I save time by skipping or combining some of the steps?

A: You're right; it is a lengthy process. But you have time because you've allotted half the time it took you to write the piece for the editing process. Even though you may be tempted to skip or combine read throughs, it's not a wise idea. You are more likely to miss errors. If you follow this process exactly, you will find the time you spent in editing was worthwhile.

Q. I'm having trouble clearing my mind for this step, and I think it's hurting my focus and objectivity. What should I do?

A. The more you can relax at this step, the better you'll be able to focus and concentrate. If soothing music or silence isn't helping you relax your mind, consider some of the following ideas:

- Put on some loose, comfortable clothing.

- Light some scented candles, spray a pleasant air freshener, or apply some scented essential oil to your pulse points. Our sense of smell is a powerful relaxation trigger. Japanese experiments have shown that the average number of errors per hour committed by keypunch operators dropped 21 percent when their air smelled of lavender, which reduces stress; 33 percent when the air was laced with jasmine, which induces relaxation; and 54 percent when the stimulating smell of lemon was present.

- Do some stretches. Loosening up your muscles can help your brain feel relaxed.

- Breathe deeply several times.

- Go for a walk. When all else fails, get up and take a brisk walk around the block or around the building. The fresh air will invigorate you, while the exercise will get your blood pumping.

Key Points

> You need to relax your mind for maximum concentration.
> Take the pressure of yourself to be perfect.
> You will need to do several read throughs to accurately locate your writing challenges.
> Skipping and/or combining steps may save you time but will hurt you in the long run.
> Find out what relaxes your mind, and then do it.

Turning Points –
Questions for Self-Reflection

Your answers to these questions will help you plan your self-editing process.

➢ Based on my self-editing checklist, I need to do _____ number of read throughs.

➢ I will plan _____ hours or _____ days to complete the read throughs.

➢ As I read my newly created text silently to myself, I feel the following about the text (the actual words):

_____

_____

_____

_____

_____

_____

_____

_____

_____

_____

_____

_____

_____

_____

_____

_____

➤ As I read my newly created text silently to myself, I feel the following about the message (the meaning and passion behind the words)

_____

_____

_____

_____

_____

_____

_____

_____

_____

_____

_____

_____

_____

_____

_____

_____

_____

➢ When I hear the words I wrote out loud, in my own voice, I feel:

_____

_____

_____

_____

_____

_____

_____

_____

_____

_____

_____

_____

_____

_____

_____

_____

_____

Step Four: Hand Off the Baton

➤ Let the Relay Begin

Use Your Team to Get Ahead

"A writer is unfair to himself when he is unable to be hard on himself."
—Marianne Moore, Poet and Pulitzer Prize Winner

You've run your segment of the race to the best of your ability. Now it's time to hand off the baton to someone else for the next leg of the race before declaring the work complete.

A lot of authors struggle with this step, because they believe writing is a solitary journey. But few things in life are accomplished without the help of others, and writing is no exception. Once you've made your writing the best you possibly can, you need to give it to someone else to make sure the writing and the piece's meaning are correct.

Writing has many facets, and they all need to merge together to make the writing effective. That's why correct writing requires the input of others; it can be to point out grammar problems, logic problems, confusing sentences, or inconsistencies in the story line. So after you've done all you can to your piece, give it to someone else and see how much better it can be.

You Can Get By with a Little Help from Your Friends

Various surveys report that 70-80% of professionals write their materials collaboratively. That is, they get input from others to make sure their writing comes across properly and professionally. The myth of the solitary author holed away in a dark, dank apartment is dead. Smart writers know they can accomplish much better results when they get outside input. Additionally, an objective outsider usually challenges us to write even better.

For many writers, handing their work off to an outsider is the scariest step. In fact, many written pieces never make it beyond a desk drawer or a computer hard drive simply because the author is too afraid to share his or her work with another person. What a shame! Who knows how many countless pieces of wonderful writing the world will never see all because of an unfounded fear.

In reality, your friends, family, and acquaintances are usually more than willing to objectively read your work and offer constructive feedback. Those who love you and care for you the most generally do want to help. All you need to do is ask.

And think about it...unless your family or friends have a "mean streak" in them, are they really going to ridicule you for writing something that has a spelling error, is a little disjointed, or perhaps loses some of its flow in a section or two? Would you ridicule them for such imperfections? Probably not. Humans, by nature, want to help each other. That's how we learn and how our species survives and thrives.

Now this doesn't mean you won't run into one or two people who will want to hamper your writing endeavors. Every family or corporate setting has at least one grumpy person who can't stand to see others succeed or follow their dreams. Chances are you know who that person is in your family or circle of influence. So simply don't ask that one person to help. You know many more people than the one grumpy soul. Focus on the 99% who want to help you, not the 1% who enjoys seeing others suffer. No matter what you do or how brilliantly you write, you'll never get constructive feedback from that negative person.

The Ground Rules

Step four of the process involves getting input from someone else to move your writing one step closer the finish line. Here are some ground rules to help you maximize your time and theirs.

☑ **Ground Rule #1:**
  Choose your team member wisely.

Rather than just give your work to anyone to read, you need to identify someone you trust. Although it may be less scary to ask a stranger to read your work (after all, you probably don't care too much what a stranger thinks of you), you need to pick someone whom you respect and who has always been supportive of you. Pick a family member, friend, or co-worker who you can trust not to squash your spirit. The wrong person can kill your desire to write again or can scare you from showing your work to anyone in the future. The last thing you want is to have this be a negative experience. So choose someone who is supportive and honest and who can empower you to keep going with your writing goals.

☑ **Ground Rule #2:**
Ask this person to read your work aloud to you.

For this step, put down your pen and paper. Fold your hands across your lap and only use your sense of hearing for this exercise. Listen to what your words sound like coming from someone else. Tape-recording yourself isn't going to cut it here. If you are listening to your voice you will still hear your inflections, your pauses, and your emphasis on certain words. Having another person read it will create some distance from your writing. You will naturally go into the role of a listener or reader, not the writer, and you will be able to easily identify awkward phrases or unclear ideas.

☑ **Ground Rule #3:**
Ask your partner to read it again.

During your partner's second read through, pick up a blank scratch pad and a pen. Don't have your actual piece in front of you. If you try to edit while your partner is reading you will get too wrapped up in one section and miss the rest. Instead, as you are listening, jot down notes about obvious mistakes you hear or items that are confusing or need more development. For example, you might write: "Point #4," "Conclusion," or "Quote in section three sounds awkward." Don't worry that your notes are too brief. When you sit down to edit your work again, your notes will jog your memory. After all, you wrote the notes and your piece.

When your partner is done reading, go back and make any necessary corrections to your document. Then print out a clean, revised copy.

☑ **Ground Rule #4:**
Ask your partner to proofread the revised copy for you.

Notice we didn't say give your partner a red pen and free reign to "correct" your writing. Instead, you want this person to proofread it. That is, indicate sections that may need some work. Your friend, family member, or co-worker is not the editor of this piece. Even if your partner is "great at writing," he or she still may not be the best editor for your particular piece. For example, a college English professor writes in a different style than a magazine editor does. Even though they are both "great at writing," they write very differently. You are the expert in knowing what your audience wants. If you let someone else correct your work, you'll never learn, so it's important to do it yourself.

Another reason to keep control of this process is that you run the risk of someone incorrectly "correcting" your writing. So don't allow your friend to actually fix your paper. Just have him or her underline, highlight, or circle confusing sections or places that have potential problems. If your friend thinks you used the wrong tense, or misspelled a word, or something was confusing, be sure he or she indicates the potential problems. When you get your piece back, carefully look at everything your friend has marked, and then decide for yourself if those items need to be changed. Finally, consider the person who proofread your document; he or she may not be familiar with the topic or may not be that skilled at editing, so don't assume the other person knows more than you. Look at every item individually.

Some Real-Life Samples

The following example shows the kind of things your partner should mark on your paper. Notice how the partner is not "correcting" the work; he or she is merely pointing things out.

Ground Rules in Action

This sample is an actual memo a client wanted to send her employees. Notice the comments from the reviewer. The person reviewing the document did not edit it; he or she merely pointed things out that the author may not have seen.

To: All employees
From: Mary Sikes
Re: Your new training assignment

Shouldn't "New Year" be in caps?

Starting with the new year, we will be doing some video training seminars in our conference room.

What language can you select to invite employees to be a part of the team so they will want to attend the training program?

The first series of the training will start on January 8, 2005. It will cover "How to Give Exceptional Customer Service." The entire video training is a series of eight tapes. They will be split over three saturdays.

Shouldn't "Saturdays" be capitalized?

Shouldn't it be a.m. and p.m.?

Everyone must participate in these sessions. They will involve watching several videos and lunch, and go from 9:30 am. to 12:00 pm. We are scheduling two groups over a period of six weeks. Group One will start on January 8th at 9:30 am. and Group Two will start on January 15th at 9:30 am. Look over the attached schedule to determine which group you are in.

Second sentence seems awkward.

What words can you choose to make employees feel this training isn't being forced down their throats?

I realize that this schedule may not work with your personal schedules. If you can't attend one of the Saturdays that you are scheduled because you have other plans outside of work, it is your responsibility to switch with someone. Also, if you are scheduled to work in the office a day that you are scheduled, you must work something out.

How can you establish a tone of excitement and enjoyment about working at ABC Company?

I am excited about this training. It will be valuable information for us to apply to our daily activities at ABC Company. Look over your schedules and let me know as soon as possible if you will be switching with someone. Thank you.

There are at least two instances where the employee is forced to "make it work" into his or her schedule.

Notice how the revised copy takes into account all the advice the reviewer offered. By pointing out the challenges, and not actually correcting them, the reviewer offered valuable insights that made the letter much stronger.

To: All employees
From: Mary Sikes
Re: Your new training assignment

I have some exciting news for everyone. With the New Year now upon us, we have an awesome opportunity to learn some new skills that will create a more harmonious work environment and better client relations.

Beginning January 8, 2005, we will be meeting for a few hours to watch some training videos, discuss the assignments, and enjoy some lunch. The entire video training is an eight-tape series, which will be split over a three-week time period. To accommodate everyone's schedule, we will be meeting in two separate groups over a six-week timeframe. Group One will start on January 8th at 9:30 a.m. and Group Two will start on January 15th at 9:30 a.m. Look over the attached schedules to determine which group you are in.

If you cannot attend one of the days you are scheduled, let's work together to find someone who can switch days with you. Also, if your work schedule conflicts with your training schedule, please let me know so we can work out an alternate plan.

I am excited about this training and know you will be too. It will provide valuable information that will help make ABC Company even better.

Frequently Asked Questions

Q: I work from home and I'm alone during the day. It's really hard for me to find someone else to help me in the editing process. Can I just record myself onto a tape player and listen to myself reading my work?

A: Yes, you can, but you won't get as much benefit as if you enlist a friend to help. When you listen to yourself reading your own work, you don't have the same emotional distance you do as when someone else is reading it. Besides, on the rare occasions you have the opportunity to hear yourself on the tape, don't you start thinking to yourself, "Do I really sound like that?" It's distracting. This is a situation where scheduling is crucial. Allow enough time for the editing process so that you can enlist the help of a friend in the evening or over the weekend. You need to make time for this step; it's that important.

Q: Should I go through this process with more than one partner?

A: You can, but it's probably not necessary unless the first person you chose turned out not to be a good pick. Some people have trouble reading aloud. Some people read aloud in monotone, some stumble over words, or just can't get into it. If you find you really didn't get what you hoped to out of the experience, pick someone else and try it again.

Q: I've thought about all my friends and family, and I've concluded that they are all mean and will all totally ridicule me for every little mistake. There's no way I can ask them to read my work. What should I do?

A: If you truly believe you can't turn to anyone within your immediate family, friend network, or circle of influence to read your work, don't despair. There is hope. Most communities have writers groups that meet regularly. You can find groups in your area by checking with local bookstores, and by scanning the community calendar of your local newspaper. Most writers groups contain both new and veteran writers. Their purpose of meeting is to share ideas, network, and offer support and encouragement to fellow authors. Join a group like this in your area. You'll likely find it a wonderful haven of supportive people who really do want you to succeed. You're sure to find someone within the group who can objectively read your work and help you with this step.

Key Points

➤ Getting outside input makes your writing stronger.

➤ Choose an editing partner whom you trust and who is supportive.

➤ Listen to your partner's input but don't take it as gospel.

➤ Community groups are a good resource to find an editing buddy.

Turning Points –
Questions for Self-Reflection

Your answers to these questions will help you plan your self-editing process.

➢ Some team members I could ask to read to my work include:

_____

_____

_____

_____

_____

_____

_____

_____

_____

_____

_____

_____

_____

_____

_____

_____

_____

_____

➢   I chose these people because:

_____

_____

_____

_____

_____

_____

_____

_____

_____

_____

_____

_____

_____

_____

_____

_____

_____

_____

➤ When I hear someone else read my work out loud I feel:

_____

_____

_____

_____

_____

_____

_____

_____

_____

_____

_____

_____

_____

_____

_____

_____

_____

➢ The differences between what I thought I had written and what I heard were:

_____

_____

_____

_____

_____

_____

_____

_____

_____

_____

_____

_____

_____

_____

_____

_____

➢ The additional writing challenges I hear rather than see at this point include:

_____

_____

_____

_____

_____

_____

_____

_____

_____

_____

_____

_____

_____

_____

_____

_____

_____

_____

Closing Thoughts

"A professional writer is an amateur who didn't quit."
–Richard Bach, American writer

A fter all your hard work and diligence, you are now approaching the finish line. You can see it up ahead, just waiting for you to cross it. This is not the time to slow down. You must push through the final steps to make it to your goal.

Unfortunately, many people quit the moment before they reach success. They feel they've done "enough," so there's no point in pushing any further. What a mistake! In an Olympic track event, one-tenth of a second is often all that separates the gold medal winner from the silver medal winner. The difference lies in that seemingly miniscule one-tenth.

When it comes to your writing and editing, don't skimp on the final one-tenth effort. This final step is where you'll find your true self-editing success.

The Ground Rule for the Last Leg of the Race

For the final step, print out your document on clean paper and read it through. If you find any additional errors that you missed in the previous steps, mark them. Be sure you're using an ink color you can easily see, such as red. Using black ink to correct your work may not be the best idea. If you make a small correction, like inserting a period or comma you omitted on page one, you may not notice the revision when you glance at that page. If your document is long, you probably won't even remember that you made a mark on page one. So make sure you use a pen color that stands out on the page.

After you mark the page, go back to your computer and make any corrections to your document. Print another clean copy and reread your paper again. If you find any mistakes, note them, go back to your computer, make the corrections, and then reprint your document. Repeat this process until you can't make any more corrections and your paper is clean. When you can read the entire document without making a single change, you have reached the goal of correctly self-editing your piece.

Now you can feel confident that when your work leaves your hands to go to your editor, your department head, or your client, that it is as close to perfection as you can get it.

 # You have now crossed the finish line. Congratulations!

Consider Your Accomplishments

Just for fun, take out the copy of your document from the very beginning of the editing process. Then take a look at your final copy. What a difference! And now think for a minute how many writers never self-edit their work; they go straight from writing it to mailing it to their editor, submitting it to their boss, or sending it to their client.

Because you took these extra steps, your work will be more polished. You will have a higher rate of publication or a greater chance for career advancement than those people who don't self-edit. You will be developing a reputation as someone who is intelligent, professional, conscientious, and creative. Editors and management will love working with you because of your finely-honed skills and dedication to the craft of writing.

Others will surely notice your advanced writing talents and will seek out your advice. You may even become an editing partner for many of your friends and co-workers.

Cross the Finish Line

With practice, this five-step self-editing process will get easier, faster, and will become second-nature to you. As a result, your work will be more accurate and have a minimum number of errors. Remember, editors don't expect your work to be 100% perfect before it gets to them, but they do expect you to be a professional writer who respects their time and who knows how to write good copy.

When you successfully follow these ground rules for self-editing, you will have mastered one of the hardest business skills—that of creating crisp, succinct, and logical written works. You will become a beloved writer to your editor and your readers as well as a valuable member to your organization. And that's the truest measure of success.

You now have the skills you need to strengthen your writing. Nothing can stop you now.

Frequently Asked Questions

Q: Isn't continually printing out my piece a waste of paper? Why can't I just reread my marked up page?

A: If you're continually reprinting a 500 page file just because you make one or two changes in the file, then yes, you are wasting paper. Only reprint the pages that you marked up and insert them into the clean pages. If you reread pages that are marked up, you'll be confusing yourself two ways: 1) the corrections will distract you when you read, possibly causing you to miss more errors; and 2) when you go back to your computer to make corrections, you're likely to miss inputting some items. You'll often think, "I already got that one last time, didn't I?" And then you'll waste more time searching for the one item to correct when you could be completing your self-editing process. So print out clean pages whenever you mark one up. Besides, filing a clean page gives you a greater sense of satisfaction.

Q: Uh-oh! I did the entire process exactly, and my editor still found some errors. What did I do wrong?"

A. Don't worry. You did nothing wrong. Remember, this is a process and will take time to master. Additionally, you're human. You're going to miss some mistakes no matter how hard you try. Ever hear the phrase "to err is human"? That's why you have editors or others to do a final approval on your work. So don't beat yourself up over it. You got your document as close to perfect as you possibly could, and that's all anyone can ask of you. Perfection simply isn't always possible. However, giving your editor a polished piece to work with is possible, and that's exactly what you did. So be proud of that!

Key Points

➢ Don't give up prior to the last step. Self-editing success is just around the corner.

➢ Always do the final read through on clean paper, and make corrections with an ink color that will stand out.

➢ Seeing the self-editing process through to completion will give you the reputation of a reliable and accurate writer.

➢ Keep practicing the skills of self-editing. Eventually it will become an automatic process that is second nature to you.

Go for the gold!

Turning Points – Questions for Self-Reflection

Your answers to these questions will help you plan your self-editing process.

➤ When I see the before and after of my written work, I feel:

_____

_____

_____

_____

_____

_____

_____

_____

_____

_____

_____

_____

_____

_____

_____

_____

_____

➤ I feel that my writing improved in the following ways:

_____

_____

_____

_____

_____

_____

_____

_____

_____

_____

_____

_____

_____

_____

_____

_____

_____

_____

➤ My new self-editing skills will help me in the following ways:

_____

_____

_____

_____

_____

_____

_____

_____

_____

_____

_____

_____

_____

_____

_____

_____

Appendices

Appendix A

What To Do When You're Pressed for Time

W e know that initially, as you're learning the self-editing process and making it a part of your writing routine, you may not have time to perform all the necessary steps. For example, your boss may walk into your office and ask you to write an announcement for the company newsletter, and then say that he needs it in twenty minutes. Or your editor may call you and ask that you get that article to her today, not next week as you had originally agreed. Or your professor may surprise you with a "pop essay quiz." These things happen, and they are simply a part of life. But just because you're pressed for time does not mean you are allowed to turn in sloppy writing. You can still self-edit successfully, no matter what the time constraints.

The Ground Rules

The following ground rules will help you when you are pressed for time.

Ground Rule #1: Forget about the clock.

Yes, that's easier said than done; however, if you focus on the time when you're editing in a crunch, you'll only make yourself nervous and more apt to miss errors. The more you can relax, the more attuned you'll be to spot your errors. So rather than glance at the clock every two minutes to see how much time you have left, turn away from the clock and don't look at it. If your deadline really is that time critical, someone will be watching the clock for you and will interrupt you when the time is up.

☑ **Ground Rule #2:**
Breathe deeply.

Rather than jump into self-editing your work in a frenzied pace, stop, take a deep breath, and then begin to edit. Again, the goal is to get your mind and body to relax. Additionally, filling your lungs with oxygen stimulates you and puts you in a better mood. The last thing you want is to edit while you're cranky.

☑ **Ground Rule #3:**
Focus on your top three writing challenges,
rather than all of them.

When time is of the essence, you may not be able to do one read through for each writing challenge on your checklist. So instead of focusing on all the challenges, only concentrate on your top three. Why? Because you make those writing mistakes more often than any others; therefore, you'll want those major problems out of your work. Yes, you'll want to catch as many of the minor problems as possible, but the minor ones likely don't happen as often. So when you're crunched for time, don't worry about them. Focus on the big stuff only.

☑ **Ground Rule #4:**
Read your text out loud, never to yourself.

When you have time to self-edit properly, you have the luxury of reading the piece to yourself several times. When you're short on time, however, you must skip this step and do all your read throughs out loud. Why? Because you want to activate both your sense of sight and hearing right away. Additionally, do as many read throughs as possible on a printed copy, not on your computer screen. That's the best way to catch the most errors.

☑ **Ground Rule #5:**
Make peace with your piece.

No written work will ever be perfect, especially if it's one you're writing when you're pressed for time. So accept this fact and move on. Anguishing over it and repeatedly telling yourself, "If I only had more time…" won't change anything. So do the best you can in the short amount of time you have, and be satisfied with your efforts.

Appendix B

How To Sabotage Your Self-Editing Efforts

Many writers inadvertently make the writing and editing process more difficult than it needs to be. As a result, they sabotage their own efforts and actually put more errors in their text than they remove.

The Ground Rules

Following are the top self-sabotaging mistakes writers make. Avoid these things and watch your self-editing success soar.

☑ **Ground Rule #1: Second-guessing yourself.**

When you second-guess yourself, you wonder if something you wrote is wrong. You may have a feeling that it's correct, but you let your self-talk convince you otherwise. You may flip-flop between right and wrong for minutes or hours. Ultimately, you decide it's wrong, when it is actually correct. Then you change the correct version to something that's incorrect. What a shame!

If you find yourself stuck in an internal struggle of whether something you wrote is correct or incorrect, more often than not, it's correct. That's right. Whatever you put on paper first comes out instinctively, and your instincts are usually right on. So if you're flip-flopping and asking yourself, "Is this right?" it probably is. Stop second-guessing yourself and focus on your proven writing challenges.

☑   Ground Rule #2: Not being willing to let go.

Some writers get so attached to their work that they're not willing to ever let it go. They're continually changing a paragraph here or refining a word choice there. Nothing they do is ever good enough, and the editing process is never-ending.

Realize that you could likely edit any piece indefinitely. You'll always find something you want to change, whether it's a single word or an entire concept. At some point you simply have to say, "That's it. It's done." And then you must hand it off. If you never let the self-editing process end, you'll never have a successful experience.

☑   Ground Rule #3: Having too many versions of the text.

Every written piece goes through many drafts. That's normal. What's not normal is saving every single version of the text you ever wrote. That's called "confusion." Even so, some writers think they must save every version "just in case." This can work if you have a good file naming system; however, most people do not. As a result, they get confused about which version of their file is the most recent, and which version they actually edited.

In reality, the only version of your text you need to save is the most recent one. If you need a part of an old version for some future writing, then save just that one part, not the entire document, and give the saved information a new file name. The more versions of your file you have, the more confusing you make the process.

☑   Ground Rule #4: Being a poor note taker.

When asked about their research materials or character background information, many writers point to their head and say, "It's all in here." They think they don't need to write out notes or keep track of facts. Then when it comes time to edit their work, they can't keep track of specifics and end up with inconsistent data and/or inaccurate information.

Realize that part of being a good writer and self-editor is having reliable data, not information you "think you know." You may need to prove something you wrote down the road, or you may need a reminder of something you said earlier in your piece. In those instances, having notes, complete with where you got the data from and how recent it is, either on paper or in your computer, are key. So learn some good note taking skills. It'll make the self-editing process much easier.

Appendix C

The Ground Rules of Grammer and Usage

Writing challenges vary greatly from person to person. When you get stuck and don't know where to turn, you can always look to a good grammar guide for reference.

"No," you say, "not the dreaded grammar guide!"

Relax. We know grammar guides can be intimidating. They're big, thick books that include every facet of grammar, and the examples are sentences you are unlikely ever to use unless you're writing scholarly works. Grammar guides have their use though. They're great when it comes to helping you identify your writing challenges. After all, knowing your challenges is half the battle.

We've compiled a short list of grammar issues that most frequently plague writers. This list is not exhaustive; it is just a starting point. When in doubt, check a grammar guide for more detailed information.

What is Grammar?

Grammar involves the form and structure of words. In popular culture, people who follow the stated writing rules practice "good" grammar. People who ignore the stated writing rules practice "bad" grammar. Usage is the way we use language, formally and informally.

Scholars have studied grammar and usage for ages. As such, they have created many grammar rules. Our intention is not to cover all of them. Instead, we've compiled a reference guide of the most popular writing challenges and quick tips for correct usage. For more detailed explanation, please consult a grammar guide.

14 Quick Grammar Tips

1. Active Versus Passive Voice

Always write with dynamic verbs. Many writers, especially those whose background is business or academics, fall into the habit of writing in the passive voice, which is not dynamic. For example, they may write: "New findings were revealed this month at the annual convention." Such a sentence structure is passive because the person or thing doing the action is not mentioned in the sentence. Instead, write, "The company president revealed new findings at the annual convention." Now you have a subject (the company president) doing the verb's action (revealing the findings). See the difference?

> ➤ **Tip:** You can spot a passive sentence by looking at the verb construction. If you have a form of the verb "to be" followed by another verb that ends in "ed" or "en" then you have a passive sentence. Here is an example of how to turn a passive sentence into an active one.
>
> The award was given to Bob. – *Passive*
> The judge gave the award to Bob. – *Active*

Review every sentence you write to make sure you are not falling into passive voice. Your readers will thank you for it.

2. Hyphen, Dash, and Ellipses

A Hyphen is one tap on the dash key, or what looks like the minus sign (–). A dash is two taps on the key, or what looks like a long minus sign (—). Ellipses is a series of three periods (...).

> ➤ Use a dash to indicate a sudden change of thought in a sentence, or before a summary of what was already stated in the sentence.

> ➤ Use a hyphen to show a break in a word, either due to the end of a line, certain compound words, or numbers.

> ➤ Use ellipses to show that words have been deleted from a passage you are quoting or to show a pause or interruption in a sentence.

Examples:

➢ **Dash**: I've always wanted to write a book—I wonder where I put my laptop—but I couldn't seem to get organized enough.

➢ **Hyphen:** My great-great-grandmother immigrated to the United States from England. She was on a boat with sixty-eight other people.

➢ **Ellipses**: I pledge allegiance to the flag...with liberty and justice for all.

3. Modifiers

Dangling modifiers are phrases that don't modify anything. What they should modify has been left out of the sentence.

☑ **Example:** Leaving the house, the front door was locked. (In this sentence, it implies that the front door left the house.)

☑ **Revised example:** Leaving the house, I locked the front door.

Misplaced modifiers are words that belong in the sentence, but are put in the wrong spot.

☑ **Example:** I read that there was a big fire in yesterday's newspaper. (In this sentence, it appears that yesterday's newspaper was on fire.)

☑ **Revised example:** I read in yesterday's newspaper that there was a big fire.

4. Number

This indicates the number of subjects that give or receive the action.

➢ **One subject:** singular noun (he, I, you)

➢ **Multiple subjects:** plural nouns (they, we, us)

5. Numbers in Text

Whether you use figures or write numbers out depends on the text. For scientific or technical writing, use figures. For less specialized writing, spell the numbers out. The following conventions apply to general writing.

Spell out numbers that can be written in one or two words.

> ☑   **Example:** Last year, only four of our eighty-seven employees used all fifteen of their paid days off.

Use figures for numbers that require more than two words to write out.

> ☑   **Example:** Julie has earned over 100,000 frequent flyer miles this year alone.

If you have to express one number in figures, write other numbers in the same sentence the same way.

> ☑   **Example:** Next year, we expect to add 20 employees to our existing staff of 453.

Spell out numbers that begin a sentence, or rewrite the sentence so the number does not come first.

> ☑   **Example:** One thousand seventy-seven people visited our web site today.

> ☑   **Revised example**: In one day our web site received 1,077 hits.

When you know the rules, the number issue is as easy as one, two, three.

6. Person

You have three choices of speakers

> ➤ **First Person:** the person speaking (I).

> ➤ **Second Person:** the person you're addressing (you).

➤ **Third Person:** the person you're talking about: (he, she or they).

7. Pronouns

To keep your writing clear, keep your pronouns close to their antecedents, or the words they refer to.

☑ **Bad example:**
As the teacher taught the child about diagramming sentences, she got tired and laid her head down on her desk. (In this sentence, you don't know whether the teacher or the student laid her head down on the desk).

☑ **Good example:**
The student got tired and laid her head down on the desk as the teacher taught her how to diagram sentences.

8. Punctuation

Most people know when to use periods, exclamation marks, and question marks, but semicolons, colons, and quotations pose greater challenges. Here are some simple rules:

Semicolon: Use it between closely related clauses in a sentence, and to join independent clauses when at least one has a comma.

For example:

- Many science classes are offered at the high school; advanced physics is the toughest.

- I'd like to go to dinner with you; however, my babysitter backed out at the last minute so I'm stuck at home.

- After I did all the research for this book, I thought I was done; but then my computer crashed.

- We went to the grocery store to buy milk, butter, and eggs; to the department store to buy sheets and towels; and to the electronics store to buy CDs, stereo equipment, and software.

Colon: Use it before items in a list and before part of a sentence that explains what was just stated.

For example:

- The things I need at the grocery store are the following: eggs, milk, bananas, cereal and orange juice.

- Jim put up a valiant fight but lost: the bear got the best of him.

Quotation marks: Quotation marks are used to indicate a speaker's exact words or to set off a definition. Single quotations set off a quote within a quote.

For example:

- The generous businessperson said, "Let's raise employee salaries by ten percent."

- My definition of a good night's rest is "eight hours of uninterrupted sleep."

- Tyler said, "I know you won't believe me, but Sarah said, 'You are a jerk.'"

9. Quotes and Punctuation

- ➢ Periods and commas always go inside quotation marks.

- ➢ Semicolon and colons go outside the quotation marks.

- ➢ Question marks, exclamation marks, and dashes go outside the quotations unless they are part of the quotation.

10. Repeating Words or Ideas Too Often in Your Text

- ➢ Repeating a word too frequently is boring and distracting. Consult your thesaurus for a comparable word, or rephrase your sentence so you don't have to use the word at all.

- ➢ Less is more. Once you explore an idea in your piece, don't keep repeating it. You will bore your readers.

➤ If you are unsure if you are using a word too frequently, use the "find" feature on your word processing program (usually under the editing taskbar). That way you will be able to find out exactly how many times you've used the same word.

11. Serial Comma

Whether or not to use the serial comma is a debate that will likely last for centuries. The publishing standard, however, says to use the serial comma before the "and" in a series. Without the serial comma, it is possible to misread the sentence, as in:

> *Robert, Bill and Jack left the house an hour ago.*

Is the above sentence stating that three men left the house an hour ago, or is it a statement to Robert that Bill and Jack left the house an hour ago? You decide.

Whenever you're listing a series of items, use the serial comma. Your readers will appreciate your ability to communicate your ideas accurately, succinctly, and coherently.

12. Spelling and Grammar

➤ Spell check can be great for typos, but it cannot pick up on the spelling of proper names, so be especially careful when spelling people's names, business names, and foreign words and locations.

➤ Watch out for homonyms (like "you're" versus "your" and "know" versus "no"). Spell and grammar check won't be able to pick up on which word you should use. The same thing goes for contractions. To make sure you're using them correctly, read the contraction as two separate words (i.e. "can not" for "can't" and "you are" for "you're").

➤ Watch for missing words. They are most often small words (like "a," "the," "an," and "or").

13. Tenses

Many writers have trouble using the correct verb tense. Boiled down to its essence, tenses come in three forms: past, present, or future tense.

> ➢ **Past tense**: I shopped at the store.

> ➢ **Present tense**: I shop at the store

> ➢ **Future**: I will shop at the store.

Make sure you keep your tense consistent throughout your text.

14. That or Which

> *This is the rule <u>that</u> people break most often.*
> *This is the rule <u>which</u> people break most often.*

Whenever you have a restrictive clause, *that* is the correct word to use. In the example above, the clause "that people break most often" is restrictive. It identifies the word "rule" and is necessary to the sentence's meaning.

> *This is the correct rule, <u>which</u> many people overlook.*
> *This is the correct rule, <u>that</u> many people overlook.*

With non-restrictive clauses, *which* is the correct word to use. Non-restrictive clauses add information to the sentence, but the content is not essential to the sentence's meaning. In the example above, the clause "which many people overlook" is non-restrictive; therefore, *which* is the correct choice.

Many people break this rule because they think *which* sounds more elegant and literary. Such people were likely raised on the British classical authors, who made no distinction between *that* and *which*. To Dickens and the Bronte sisters, *that* was a word for the meager class.

Alas, the grammar rules for American English preach that we should use *that* for restrictive clauses and *which* for non-restrictive ones. Remember, it's the house "*that* Jack built," not "*which* Jack built."

If you can't tell whether a clause is restrictive or non-restrictive, use the comma as your guide. When a comma seems appropriate before the clause, it's probably non-restrictive. Use *which*. When the comma seems intrusive, it's most likely restrictive. Use *that*.

This is one rule *that* you can live by.

22 Quick Usage Tips

1. Address the reader directly.

For example, "*You* will discover that..." "You" is the most powerful word to a reader. If you had a friend named Dan and you were having a conversation with him, you'd call him by name. It's the same thing with your readers. But since you don't know your reader's first name, use the next best thing: "you."

2. Avoid negative sentence constructions.

Not "Your business will not suffer," but "Your business will prosper." While a business not suffering is a positive, it's a backhanded positive. It's kind of like telling your girlfriend, "No. That dress doesn't make you look *that* fat." Even better, show the results, don't tell. What does a prosperous business look like? Describe the happy employees, rising profits, and satisfied customers—all of which are signs of prosperity.

3. Be super fussy about finding the right word.

Choose specific and concrete words that best get your points across. Be aware of the word's sound, its rhythm, and its connotation, as well as its dictionary meaning.

> ➤ Watch synonyms: Even though two words are synonyms, they often evoke different images. For example, consider the words "compliant," "agreeable," and "willing." While they all refer to generally the same thing, they have different connotations. So before you just pick a word at random and think it's a synonym, carefully analyze the word's connotation.

> ➤ Choose appropriate words: Choose words that are honest, specific, and plain, and that give the reader the effect you want. Don't just try to impress your readers by using big words. Capture the meaning you want with the simplest and fewest words possible. So don't write, "Due to the fact of the

situation caused by the president of the company…" write, "Because of the situation the company president caused…" The first sentence uses fourteen words, the second says the same thing in eight words.

4. Close with emotion.

Don't leave readers flat. Whatever you write has to come to a natural close that wraps up all the information you've just given. Make sure your close has some sort of Call to Action—what do you want people to do or think as a result of reading this piece? Do you want them to call you? Do you want them to change some aspect of their business? Actually say it. If you're writing a sales piece, such as a brochure, say "Call ABC Company today for your free estimate." If you're writing a magazine article and want people to employ your success strategies, say, "Use these strategies today to reap greater profits tomorrow." Don't make readers read between the lines. Tell them what you want.

5. Evoke images.

Instead of "The house across the street," write "The two-story Victorian by the fork in Smithfield Road." Evoke more than one of the five senses when you write. If you're a candy manufacturer, make your readers taste the candy. If you're a florist, make your readers smell the flowers, not just see what they look like. If you're talking about business productivity, make your readers hear the hustle of productivity and feel the rush of a sales call. Do more than just tell them what's going on.

6. Include conflict.

People love conflict. They love to take sides and they love to debate. If you can show some conflict in your piece, you'll draw people in.

7. Keep the reader emotionally involved.

You can use one of three great ways to do this:

> ➤ Present and unravel a mystery. It can be something as simple as "Have you ever wondered why some company leaders have great media exposure while others who run a similar business can barely get a producer or editor to take notice?" Then you unravel that mystery by showing why that happens and how to change it.

➤ Create a situation of jeopardy and resolve it. Show readers what could go wrong and what they need to do to resolve it. For example: "Your home is your place of comfort and refuge. However, during a tornado, it can be flattened in an instant. That's why steel-reinforced rooms are a necessity for people living in tornado-prone areas."

➤ Identify a problem readers can relate to and solve it. Know what issues your readers are facing and use it as an example. As in: "With more and more organizations laying off staff, slashing budgets, and reorganizing departments in an attempt to cut costs and increase cash flow, many company leaders struggle as they attempt to do more with less." Then go into strategies for solving the presented problem.

8. Make a major point, step away from it, and return with force.

Think of it as the one-two punch of writing. Don't lay it all on them at once. Give them a taste to pique their interest, then back away, then entice them again, this time giving the full story. It's like letting your dog smell the bone and maybe lick it, but then taking it away. A few moments later you give the dog the bone and now he wants it more than ever. So if you're giving a strategy in your writing. You may say what it is and the benefit quickly, such as "Yield nine percent interest in six months with no risk." But then you back off and maybe explain why such a rate of return is near impossible to get. Then you come back to what the readers really want—the info on the no risk investment.

9. Make your sentences rise to a climax.

Then, let them reveal their significant emotion at the end. Do the same with paragraphs. Support your general ideas with examples. Arrange your thoughts in ascending order of importance, saving the best for last. Just as a trial attorney can't pull questions or a hypothesis out of thin air, neither can you. You must build up to that grand thought and make it your piece's moment of climax.

Experiment with your sentences. Change the position or order of key phrases and listen to the difference. Change the sentence's rhythm and cadence. Experiment with the effect of repeating similar strong beginning for a series of sentences, or for similar strong endings. Break out of the usual writing rut.

10. Plant questions throughout the piece.

As you answer one, pose another. This will keep people's curiosity engaged. These don't have to be blatant questions, as in "Why do people
behave this way?" They can be subtle questions that your writing evokes.
You can explain a situation that will prompt the reader to question him
or herself, "Hmmm. I wonder why people behave that way?" Then you
answer it.

11. Promise to reveal something exciting soon.

This works best for sales letters and sales oriented pieces. You've read
pieces like this, "In the next few pages you'll learn the exciting secrets
to weight loss and longevity."

12. Reach for the unexpected, surprising word, phrase, image, or sentence.

Give readers something different, not the same stuff they can read anywhere else. The bottom line is that if you want people to invest the time
and money to read your work, you have to tell them something new.
While you should use other people's works to substantiate claims or add
credibility to your message, make sure your central idea is fresh and
unique. To make your approach new, incorporate the results of a survey
you personally conducted, or include case studies from your business or
life. Interview people who can contribute pertinent facts and information.
This is your book, so tell your story or stance on an issue.

> ➢   **Tip**: People like controversy. If your written piece
>   can stir things up and make people think twice about
>   something, you'll have a greater chance of creating
>   a buzz about your work.

13. Shift emotion in the middle of a sentence.

For example, "Most people claim to enjoy this service, but candid
interviews reveal otherwise." This gives readers the surprise element they
love, as it plays with their emotions. And when you can evoke emotion
of any kind, you'll catch people's attention. We as humans do this all the
time. How many times have you said to someone, "I'm really happy to
see you," and then immediately thought to yourself, "No. No I'm not."
Emotion keeps people involved in your text.

14. Start with a statement of fact.

Then prove it with details. Justify what you say with logic. Make sure every paragraph has a topic sentence and that every other sentence in the paragraph supports that point.

15. Use a series of short sentences with strong verbs to build tension.

This will keep your readers on edge and anxious to read more. For a piece about stress you may write an intro that goes like this: "You're in your office scrambling to finish a project. In walks your boss. He drops another project on your desk. It's due today. In 2 hours. Then the phone rings. It's your son. He has bad news…"

16. Use action for important points.

Instead of "She was shocked," write, "Her eyes bulged and her jaw was agape." Paint pictures with your words. Help your readers visualize the scene you're painting for them. Contrary to popular belief, the best writers think in pictures, not words. See the image in your mind, and then write what you see.

17. Use grace notes, asides, or actions that add emotion, color, and intimacy to your writing.

Every once in a while, section some part of the text in parenthesis to act as an aside to the readers. Use comparisons, contrasts, metaphors, similes, and analogies to sharpen your meaning. Remember, a comparison likens one object to a similar object, as in "She acts just like her mother." That comparison becomes a simile when the two objects being compared are by nature dissimilar, as in "She acts like a mother hen." A comparison becomes a metaphor when the two objects are equated and not compared, as in "She is the mother to us all," rather than "She is like a mother to us." Actual motherhood is beside the point; figurative motherhood is being evoked.

18. Use parallelism for emphasis and rhythm.

"…that this government of the people, by the people, for the people…" "I came; I saw; I conquered." Much of the power of writing comes from the repetition of words and phrases and the connection made between them. Martin Luther King Jr.'s "I Have a Dream" speech is the perfect example of parallelism. He begins every paragraph of the speech with the phrase "I have a dream." Devices like these are most useful when you are writing with strong emotion. They give form to passion without softening the message.

19. Vary the lengths of sentences and paragraphs.

Just as many short sentences create tension, many long sentences put people in a logical state of mind. So you want to intermingle short and long sentences to show readers the ups and downs and all the emotions in between.

20. Write colloquially when appropriate.

If you're too formal, you'll lose your readers. Have you ever reread your own work only to declare, "It sounds all wrong!"? That's because the tone of your writing was all wrong.

> **Tip**: Different types of writing require different tones. A business letter should not have the same tone as a love letter, and an article on Information Technology would have a different tone if it's intended for a technical journal or a mass-market magazine.

In non-fiction writing, the three most common inappropriate tones are:

> **Excessive formality** – This occurs often when a writer is insecure about his or her authority and tries to mask it by using too many large words, long sentences, and technical terms. Of course, if the intended audience is technical, it's appropriate to use technical terms, but using the same terms for lay readers will leave them unimpressed and bored.

> **Out of place humor** – Out-of-place humor also comes from insecurity and the author's need for approval. While there is nothing wrong with a humorous outlook, if you are joking simply to win over your readers, your humor will backfire. The same can be said for sarcasm and irony. When done appropriately and for the correct audience, humor, sarcasm, and irony can make your point; however, when done gratuitously, they can go misunderstood.

➢ **Misdirected anger** – Anger, no matter how justified, is rarely persuasive. For example, an angry argument for or against an issue may move the readers who already share your view to action but it may also alienate those you wish to persuade. Anger can quickly get in the way.

21. Write in the present or simple past tense when possible.

Instead of writing, "Studies have proven," write, "Studies prove…" Or, write in simple past. This is when you take the root verb and add "ed," such as "Studies proved," "The business prospered," and "I played." These tenses keep the action moving.

22. Write to a specific audience.

Be friendly and concerned for your reader's welfare. Always prove to your readers that you have their best interest in mind and that nothing you write is self-serving. For example, you may write, "When touring the Smithsonian, be sure to visit the American sculptors exhibit (arrive early for the shortest lines)." Make your readers feel that they're getting insider secrets and great value for their investment in reading your words. Give your readers the same insider information you'd give your best friend.

Appendix D

Forms and Checklists

Following are some forms and checklists that will help you on your self-editing journey. Feel free to photocopy these and use them as necessary. For a blank downloadable version of these forms and checklists, please go to www.cameopublications.com/forms.

Example: Self-Editing Checklist

Challenge	% of Occurrence	Comments
Passive sentence construction	50%	In business school, we learned to write in passive voice. Readers find that boring. Keep my writing active so people actually read my documents.
Wordiness	30%	Write what I want in as few words as possible. Readers don't want to be impressed with my big sentences. They want to understand a complex topic. Continually ask myself, "Do I really need that word or phrase?"
Redundant sentence structures	10%	Vary my sentence structure so my writing is more interesting to read.
Possessive nouns	5%	I often get possessive and plural mixed up. Rather than just always use an apostrophe, look to see if the noun in the sentence is showing ownership.
Semicolons	5%	A semicolon is a stronger pause than a comma, but a weaker pause then a period. Use a semicolon to join related ideas.

Self-Editing Checklist

Challenge	% of Occurrence	Comments

Self-Editing Checklist

Challenge	% of Occurrence	Comments

Self-Editing Checklist

Challenge	% of Occurrence	Comments

Self-Editing Checklist

Challenge	% of Occurrence	Comments

Writing Challenges Checklist

Having trouble figuring out what to even look for in your writing? Here is a list of some of the most common writing challenges that plague writers. This list is not all-inclusive; it simply lists the most common writing challenges we see people have.

- ➢ Awkward sentence construction
- ➢ Dangling modifiers
- ➢ Disorganized text
- ➢ Faulty logic
- ➢ Ideas not fully developed
- ➢ Incorrect verb form
- ➢ Lack of variety in sentence structure
- ➢ Misplaced modifiers
- ➢ No topic sentence in paragraphs
- ➢ No transitions between thoughts
- ➢ Passive sentence construction
- ➢ Possessive versus plural
- ➢ Redundancies
- ➢ Run on sentences
- ➢ Semicolon misuse
- ➢ Sentence fragments
- ➢ Spelling
- ➢ Subject – verb agreement
- ➢ Wordiness

The Self-Editing Process at a Glance

You can find more blank forms at www.cameopublications.com/forms.
(Check off each item as you complete it.)

Never miss a step! Following is the self-editing process at a glance. Use this handy list to jog your memory of what to do next during every self-editing session.

- ☐ Search for the Occurrence of Similar Errors

- ☐ Build a Personalized Editing Checklist

- ☐ Make Time for the Editing Phase

- ☐ Get Into an Editor's Mindset

- ☐ Detach From Your Work

- ☐ Work on a Hard Copy

- ☐ Make Several Passes Through Your Text to Look for a Specific Issue

- ☐ Ask Somebody Else to Read Your Work Aloud to You

- ☐ Ask a Friend to Proofread the Work for You

- ☐ Finally! Print Your Work on Clean Paper and Give it One Last Read-Through

Epilogue

"Happiness comes when your work and words are of benefit to yourself and others."
–Buddha

Writing and editing a work about any topic is difficult. Writing and editing a book about writing and editing is a daunting task, to say the least. However, with so many people who write in today's society—those who write "professionally" as well as those who write as part of their profession—we knew we needed to share these strategies with our fellow writers. After all, simply knowing how to do something is not enough. Transferring that knowledge to others is the true sign of mastery.

As you use this self-editing process, you may initially struggle. And that's okay. Any change to an ingrained habit or routine causes some discomfort. They key is to stick with it, for in the end, your writing will improve, and you will gain credibility in whatever topic you choose to write about.

Also realize that studies show it takes, on average, twenty-eight days to develop a new habit. So stick with this process for at least a month. Only then will the steps become second nature so you can write stronger, more powerful text.

Author T.S. Elliot once said that his editor, Ezra Pound, was his best friend. When you break self-editing down into these five simple steps, you will be your own best friend because you'll be able to effectively edit your own work.

Remember, with practice, self-editing will get easier and faster and become part of your writing routine. When it does, you'll reap the greatest rewards. While no one is perfect, when you follow these ground rules and this self-editing process, you can be confident that your work is the best it can possibly be.

Best of luck in all your editing pursuits!

Index

A

active voice 55, 56, 106
adverb versus adjective use 38
American English 112
attachment to written work 23, 52
audience 80, 118, 119
audience, intended 118

B

Bach, Richard 91
breathe deeply 102
Buddha 127

C

call to action 26, 114
Capote, Truman 15
checklist 53, 55, 56, 57, 71, 74
choose a team member, how to 19, 78, 86
climax in sentences 115
College Board's National Commission on Writing 15
colon 109, 110
comparison 117
conflict in text 114, 115
contrast 117
Cormier, Robert 67
creativity, with writing 22, 45

D

dangling modifiers 39, 107
dash 106, 107, 110
data entry
dictionary 17, 70, 71, 113
double negative 38, 40

E

editing 15, 17, 18, 45, 51, 52, 53, 54, 55
editing checklist 53, 55, 56, 57, 74
editing checklist, sample 55, 56
editor 16, 22, 45, 51, 52, 53, 54, 60, 68, 71, 80, 92, 93, 114
editor's mindset 52, 54, 61, 66, 68
Elliot, T.S. 127
ellipses 106, 107
emotion 115, 116, 117, 118
emotion, close with 114
emotion, reader involved 114
emotional distance, from work 79, 83
emotion in writing 116
evoke images 114
excessive formality 118

F

feedback, constructive 22, 49, 78
first person 108
fresh eye, for editing 54, 60

G

grammar 13, 17, 22, 25, 45, 46, 54, 70, 77, 105, 111, 112
grammar, difficulty of 105
grammar check 45, 111
grammar guides 17, 18, 25, 105
grammar guides, benefits of 105
grammar guides, problem with 17, 105
grammar tips 106

H

hard copy 54, 60
Hemingway, Ernest 21
hiring editors 60
homonym confusion 40, 41
humor, out of place 118

hyphen 106, 107

K

keystrokes, errors 67
King Jr, Dr. Martin Luther 118

L

listening 79

M

margin notes 23, 26
mental blocks 52
metaphor 117
mindset for self-editing 52, 54, 66, 68
misplaced modifiers 41, 107
modifiers 32, 107
Moore, Marianne 77

N

negative sentence construction 113
note taker 104
numbers 106, 107, 108
numbers, in text 108

O

objectivity in editing 52, 54, 61, 68, 71
organization; in writing 23, 26, 55, 57

P

parallelism 38, 40, 117, 118
parenthesis 117
passion for writing 52, 61, 75, 118
passive voice 30, 39, 41, 43, 53, 55, 56,
    57, 70, 106
Pound, Ezra 127
preparation for self-editing 21, 51, 53,
    61
pronouns 109
proofread 80
punctuation 37, 39, 41, 42, 43

Q

Quintilanus, Marcus Fabius 51
quotation marks 110
quotes and punctuation 110

R

read through 68, 71, 72, 74
reading aloud 83, 102
relaxation techniques 72
Repeating Words 110
repetition, in writing 24, 32, 41, 42, 117
run-on sentence 38, 41

S

sales letters 116
schedule, sample 55, 58
second-guessing 103
second person 108
self-editing, definition of 16
self-editing checklist, example of 121
self-editing fears 17
self-editing process 16, 17, 18, 91, 92,
    93, 98, 127
semi colon 56, 109, 110
sentence structure 24, 45, 46, 56, 106
serial comma 111
simile 117
spelling 37, 39, 45, 53, 55, 70, 71, 78,
    111
spell check 111
statement of fact 117
subject/verb agreement 37, 40

T

tenses 17, 53, 80, 112, 119
tense shift 42
that vs. which 42, 112, 113
thesaurus 17, 70, 71, 110
third person 109
time, scheduling for self-editing 53, 54
time management 53, 101
topic sentence 24, 30, 117

typos 111

U

usage 17, 105, 113

W

which vs. that 112, 113
wordiness 32, 37, 40, 56
writer's groups 83
writer's mindset 52, 54, 66, 68
writer (vs. editor) 51, 52, 53, 54, 61,
        66, 68
writing, reflection of you 22
writing, types of 118
writing challenges, personalized 17, 21,
        22, 23, 25, 46, 51, 53, 55, 57, 63,
        68, 70, 72, 90, 102, 105
writing feedback 22, 49, 78
writing skills, importance of 15
writing well, definition of 15

About Dawn Josephson

Dawn Josephson,The Master Writing Coach,™ empowers leaders to master the printed word for enhanced credibility, positioning, and profits. Through one-on-one coaching, dynamic keynotes, and informational workshops, Dawn teaches clients how to write irresistible books, articles, and marketing pieces that position them as the expert. She also assists with idea development for written works.

Dawn got her first piece published at age 8. Today she has over 1500 published articles and 20 published books to add to her list of accomplishments, many of which are published under her clients' names. Her client list includes high-ranking political attorneys, Ivy League college professors, CEOs and executives of major corporations, and professional speakers awarded both CSP and CPAE designations.

As a speaker, Dawn delivers entertaining and thought-provoking presentations on various aspects of writing. In addition to coaching and speaking, Dawn is also a savvy business professional. She is founder and president of Cameo Publications, LLC, an editorial and publishing services firm located on Hilton Head Island, SC, and is the creator of The Ground Rules™ book series. Before founding Cameo Publications in 1998, Dawn worked as Editor-in-Chief for a national magazine publisher, an editorial consultant for book publishers, a regularly contributing writer to arts and entertainment magazines, an ad copywriter for small and mid-sized businesses, and a technical writer for a software company.

Dawn is a member of Publisher's Marketing Association, Who's Who Among Entrepreneurs, the National Association of Women Writers, and the National Speakers Association. As a result of her hard work and creativity, Dawn has been appointed Chair of the National Speakers Association Writer's and Publisher's Professional Expert Group for the 2005/2006 year.

Dawn is a recognized expert in her field and is known for her straightforward writing, humor, and bold approach. She has been featured in such media outlets as Investor's Business Daily, PR News, HR Magazine, Job Placement & Training Report, Educational Dealer, Real Estate Broker's Insider, Writer's Weekly, and other national publications.

Dawn's internationally acclaimed book, *Putting It On Paper: The Ground Rules for Creating Promotional Pieces that Sell Books*, is a valuable tool for authors to more effectively market their books.

About Lauren Hidden

 **Lauren Hidden** is the founder of The Hidden Helper, L.L.C. Begun in 2003, her business helps entrepreneurs increase their productivity by allowing them to focus on the tasks that are most enjoyable and profitable to them. The Hidden Helper provides editorial and virtual assistance services, including writing, editing, proofreading, research, transcription, real estate support, and virtual office management. Her clients include professional speakers, authors, real estate professionals, and entrepreneurs in a variety of fields.

Before founding her own company, Lauren gained her editorial experience by working as the Communications Coordinator for a Fortune 500 company, a county caseworker for the elderly, and a freelance writer and researcher. With The Hidden Helper, Lauren has blended her communications skills with her desire to help others.

Lauren is a graduate of Shippensburg University with a B.A. in Communications/Journalism and an interdisciplinary concentration in Sociology.

Lauren is an active member of the International Virtual Assistants Association and the Delaware Valley Virtual Assistants Association.

Visit The Hidden Helper on the web at http://www.hiddenhelper.com or email her at Lauren@hiddenhelper.com

Put The Ground Rules to Work at Your Next Event!

Dawn Josephson is a presenter on the following:

➤   Popular Business Writing Presentations:

Writing for Profit – By simply enhancing the writing skills of you and your employees, you can increase profits by at least 20%. Learn how to develop and teach employee writing guidelines specific to your company's needs and clientele.

Words That Sell – Sure, the English language contains hundreds of thousands of words, but only 21 of them can easily sell your clients. Learn what they are and how to use them so you can save both time and money when selling to prospects.

Get to the Point Quickly and Effectively – Now you can master the 10 principles of effective written business communication. Learn what these principles are and how to best utilize them in all your company's written materials, from sales literature to client correspondence.

Pitch Yourself on Paper – When you're writing a business proposal, how you pitch your company, your ideas, your products, or your services makes the difference between success and failure. Without a powerful pitch, even the most brilliant message can fall on deaf ears. Learn how to create a professional pitch that showcases your company's talents and your product or service's benefits.

➤   Popular Author Presentations:

Write to Sell! How to Create Promotional Pieces that Sell Books Authors who have an effective book press kit sell more books. Even if your book has mass appeal, a well-crafted book press kit will help you gain the attention of the media, bookstores, and distribution houses. Now you can learn the essential press kit secrets that lead to success.

Make Your Writing Irresistible – If you want publishers and readers to buy your work, you need to write in a way that's both engaging and informative. Sure, you may be able to tell a good story, but if your writing isn't absolutely irresistible, it may miss the mark. Now you can give your writing the sparkle and pizzazz that lead to increased sales.

What Every Writer Needs to Know to Build a Satisfying Writing Career – Go from good to great! Now you can discover the secrets successful writers use to become household names and stay that way. This program will show new and veteran writers how to take their writing career to the next level. Participants will learn foolproof ways to get ahead when the competition is fierce.

To book **Dawn Josephson** for your next conference or event, call 1-866-372-2636 or send an e-mail to dawn@masterwritingcoach.com or visit www.masterwritingcoach.com.

➤ Additional Resources

To receive a discount on any of these reports, subscribe to Cameo Publications' E-tips or call 843-785-3770. Log on to www.cameopublications/writerstools. com for more infromation.

☐ **5 Most Overlooked Rules for Outstanding Writing** – Get readers interested in your work by utilizing these 5 rules. You will forge deeper connections with your readers and reap more sales. E-Report $ 5.00 Automatic Download

☐ **21 Words that Sell** – Take the copy in your brochures, proposals, and ads up a notch by including these words. This report also includes a free downloadable list of the 21 words. E-Report $ 7.00 Automatic Download

☐ **24 Tips for More Lively Writing** – Master the techniques that make readers eager to read your words. Add excitement and drama to everything you write. E-Report $ 7.00 Automatic Download

☐ **Create a Powerful Book Press Kit** – Learn how to create a book press kit that gets your book media exposure and in bookstores and distribution houses. E-Report $ 7.00 Automatic Download

☐ **Create Sensational Titles** – Draw your readers into your work in 5 seconds or less. Learn the formulas for creating titles that work—hook line, and sinker. E-Report $ 5.00 Automatic Download

☐ **Elevate Your Message with Quality Research** – Learn how to find reliable and credible sources that can substantiate your message. Never have your words be misproven again. E-Report $ 7.00 Automatic Download

☐ **Excite Your Readers with What They Want** – Discover how to give readers the information they truly want, rather than what you think they need. Build a loyal base of readers who seek our your work. E-Report $ 5.00 Automatic Download.

☐ **Get Your Book Featured in Top Publications: A Magazine Editor Tells All!** – A former magazine editor gives you the inside scoop on how to work with editors and producers to get your book the media exposure it deserves. Learn the little-known phrases editors love to hear. E-Report $7.00 Automatic Download.

☐ **Overcome Writer's Block** – Never fear the blank computer screen again. Now you can get your creative juices flowing when the words simply won't come. E-Report $5.00 Automatic Download.

Also Available from Dawn Josephson:

Make Your Writing Irresistible to Attract More Readers, audio CD
> Learn how to connect with your readers and write in a way that leaves them enthralled with your work. Dawn Josephson shows you how to develop a reader-focus for your writing, help your readers see themselves in your text, eliminate the deadwood that bogs readers down, and meet your readers' expectations every time. $69.

So You Wanna Be a Ghostwriter: How Make Money Writing Without a Byline, E-report
> Many freelance writers find it difficult to break into the publishing world. What they don't know, however, is that there's a faster and easier way to see their words in print. It's called ghostwriting, and it's an extremely lucrative, fun, and challenging career. Learn how to break into this field and succeed. $10.

Secrets and Strategies for Powerful Writing CD-ROM
> Fifteen insider reports that will help you become a better writer, faster and easier than ever before. Learn how to overcome writer's block, how to self-edit like a pro, how to make your writing lively, plus much more. $50.

Quick Order Form

Fax orders: 843-785-8722. Send this form.

Telephone orders: Call 1-866-37-CAMEO (372-2636) toll free. Have your credit card handy.

Secure Online Ordering: www.cameopublications.com

Postal Orders: Cameo Publications, PO Box 8006, Hilton Head Island, SC 29938-8006, USA. Telephone: 843-785-3770

☐ *Make Your Writing Irresistible to Attract More Readers,* audio CD $69.

☐ *So You Wanna Be a Ghostwriter: How Make Money Writing Without a Byline* E-Report $10. No Shipping

☐ *Secrets and Strategies for Powerful Writing* CD-ROM $50.

Please send more FREE infromation on:
☐ Other books ☐ Tele-Seminars ☐ Speaking/Seminars ☐ Consulting

Name: _____

Address: _____

City: _____ State:___ Zip: _____

Phone _____ Email (optional) _____

☐ YES! - I want the FREE Cameo Insider E-Tips.

Card # _____

Name on card _____ Exp date: _____

Shipping:
USA: $4.95 for first item; add $2.00 for each additional book
SC residents please include 5% sales tax.

Book Order Form

Fax orders: 843-785-8722. Send this form.

Telephone orders: Call 1-866-37-CAMEO (372-2636) toll free. Have your credit card handy.

Secure Online Ordering: www.cameopublications.com

Postal Orders: Cameo Publications, PO Box 8006, Hilton Head Island, SC 29938-8006, USA. Telephone: 843-785-3770

#

☐

Write It Right:
The Ground Rules
for Self-Editing Like the Pros
$17.95

ISBN: 0-97449662-6

☐

Putting It On Paper:
The Ground Rules for Creating Promotional
Pieces That Sell Books
$19.95

ISBN: 0-9744966-1-8

Order Total _____

Please send more FREE infromation on:

☐ Other books   ☐ Tele-Seminars   ☐ Speaking/Seminars   ☐ Consulting

Name: _____

Address: _____

City: _____ State: ___ Zip: _____

Phone _____ Email (optional) _____

Shipping:
USA: $4.95 for first item; add $2.00 for each additional book
SC residents please include 5% sales tax.

Card # _____

Name on card _____ Exp date: _____

To book Dawn Josephson for your conference or event call
1-866-372-2636 or email Dawn@masterwritingcoach.com